The
Fearless Fish
Out of Water

HOW TO SUCCEED
WHEN YOU'RE THE
ONLY ONE LIKE YOU

Robin Fisher Roffer

John Wiley & Sons, Inc.

Published by John Wiley & Sons, Inc., Hoboken, New Jersey.
Published simultaneously in Canada.

For general information on our other products and services or for technical support, please contact our Customer Care Department within the United States at (800) 762-2974, outside the United States at (317) 572-3993 or fax (317) 572-4002.

Wiley also publishes its books in a variety of electronic formats. Some content that appears in print may not be available in electronic books. For more information about Wiley products, visit our web site at www.wiley.com.

Library of Congress Cataloging-in-Publication Data:

Roffer, Robin Fisher, 1962-
    The fearless fish out of water : how to succeed when you're the only one like you / Robin Fisher Roffer.
        p. cm.
    Includes bibliographical references and index.
    ISBN 978-0-470-31668-9 (cloth)
        1. Success in business.   2. Success.   3. Career development.   4. Self-realization.
    I. Title.
    HF5386.R543 2009
    650.1–dc22   2008037686

Printed in the United States of America

10   9   8   7   6   5   4   3   2   1

Contents

Acknowledgments

To the most Fearless Fish I know
I dedicate this book to my daughter
ROXY
and my husband,
STEVEN ROFFER,
who keeps it real each and every day.
And to my father
ROBERT J. EDELMAN
who fearlessly raised two girls on his own.
I give my love and appreciation
to my best friend and sister,
WENDY HARDMAN
I am blessed with a fantastic agent and cheerleader,
MEL BERGER
and a soulful and gifted collaborator,
DAVID CHRISTAL.
For supporting my spiritual quest
and showing me the meaning of true friendship,
SEDENA and GEORGE CAPPANNELLI
DEBORAH and MATTHEW MITCHELL.

I'd also like to give my heartfelt thanks
to my friends and business associates
who bravely showed me the way
SUSAN O'MEARA,
HAROLD "H" LEWIS,
GRACIELA MEIBAR,
JAY CORSON,
TESSA GOLDSTON,
and the woman who put me on the path
KIM YOUNGBLOOD.

Introduction

Being different is good. That's what I believe. But like many of us growing up, I was told "children should be seen and not heard," "don't rock the boat," and "try to fit in." Today, the messages are more inclusive. We live in the "Gilded Age of Children," where kids play in a Disney-walled garden that encourages all kinds of flowering and frowns on any kind of prejudice.

As a result, there's a battle cry for authenticity in action, being your own person, and expressing your true self. From building Facebook pages, to programming our DVRs, to customizing the ringtones on our cell phones—individualizing is everywhere. People want to do it *their* way; and yet that driving force to fit in with the group is still strong. As a result, the ones that look, think, or act in a unique way are sometimes not invited to meetings, ignored at gatherings, denied plum projects, and passed up for promotions. The irony is that almost all of us at one point or another have felt outside the circle or out of step with everyone else.

You may be someone who attracts attention. Maybe you're a college graduate in your first job. Maybe you're the only woman of color on the board. Maybe you have a strong accent; you're from a different country and you're trying to make it in a foreign culture. Maybe your colleagues are on their BlackBerrys, while you still have a Day Planner and think that "IM" is missing an apostrophe. You're different from everyone. *You're a fish out of water.*

I know what it's like. I've been a fish out of water my whole life. And I know what it can do *for* you. My aim in writing this book is to show people who are outside the circle—because of gender, race, age, style, attitude, or any other factor—how to make it to the top; not in spite of their differences, but *because* of them. Being different is a powerful position if you know how to use it.

Back in my corporate days, I remember Monday mornings and that 9 o'clock meeting looming as I'd hurry to work. I couldn't be one minute late—I was a woman and one of the youngest directors in the company. My boss knew what I could do—he hired me, he had confidence—but *I'd* always wonder if I belonged there. *Everyone seemed to be in the swim except me.*

Chances are during your career you've been the only person like you in a room. You've felt left out, undervalued, unheard, ineffective, or misunderstood. You were a fish out of water; maybe because of your values, maybe because of your circumstances. You might be someone who has worked hard for everything you have and you're surrounded by co-workers who have had it all handed to them. Or maybe you're the creative maverick bumping into walls in a corporate environment. Whatever the case, you feel outside the circle because you're different. How do you get inside when your differences keep you on the periphery?

As a fish out of water myself, I know that the very things that set you apart can take you exactly where you want to be. When you focus on the positive aspects of your differentness, instead of trying to blend—your success has the potential to be unbounded. This book will show you how to live your truth and have it all.

The following seven career-tested steps will give you the motivation and inspiration to turn your uniqueness into an advantage. You'll learn to recognize the strengths that your differences give you and understand the secrets for positioning them to work for you. The personal stories of other Fearless Fish out of water—taken from interviews I have conducted with many successful people in business, law, entertainment, and other industries—will show the way, along with the easy-to-follow guidelines and engaging exercises I provide in each step.

This book will give hope to those who wonder if they can make it when they're not like everyone else. It will show you that you can be exactly who you are, live more deeply, and have a more rewarding career—all at the same time. That's one of the secrets to success for the fish out of water: Be *more* of who you are. When you give the world an authentic representation of the real you, you'll find acceptance and even admiration. You'll be a part of it all—*without* losing yourself.

Standing out can be lonely. It has its challenges. But it's also an exceptional opportunity. Bob Dylan, Oprah, and Steve Jobs are just a few well-known personalities who were definitely not voted "most popular" in their graduating classes. But they never let others' views of them hold them back.

This book is the permission slip to celebrate your unique style. Here are the insider secrets to doing it *your* way and living big!

Step

Go Fishing for the Real You

Fearless Fish Out of Water
Accept Who They Are

- Open up to your authentic self.
- Free yourself from the desire to conform.
- Make a great first impression.
- Bust the myths about you.
- Accept yourself and others will follow.

Back in the day, I used to talk way too much (some would argue that I still do!). The more nervous I got, the more I would blabber on. Because this habit didn't come from a place of strength, others would see me as inauthentic—and, let's face it, exhausting. This need to be heard was just one of the self-protections that had become part of my identity. I grew up entertaining my single father after dinner by performing song and dance shows for him in the living room. Getting his attention was getting his love; and nothing meant more to me. Years later, on a second date with the man I would one day marry, he interrupted me as I regaled him with stories from my youth. "Will the real Robin Fisher please stand up?" he asked. I burst into tears. No one had ever called me on my act before! I felt exposed, unsure of what to do next, where moments earlier I'd felt confident and charming. I wanted to secure his interest, and I didn't know how else to get it. This experience was the turning point that showed me that I don't need to entertain to be appreciated. Friends helped cement the message, telling me how happy they were to finally feel I was letting them get to know the real me; and I, too, enjoyed our friendships more.

So many of us continue our childhood roles into our adult life, only to find that they don't work anymore. Maybe you've been knocking yourself out to earn approval or worrying obsessively about money because growing up your family always felt the lack. Sometimes it takes a wake-up call like mine to realize that operating as in the past or out of fear is a failed strategy.

None of us comes into this world with a handbook to guide us in developing our personalities. We simply jump into life and do the best we can. But what if you feel different—that you somehow don't fit in with the norm, that you aren't truly recognized and accepted for who you are?

Trying to retrofit yourself into society and work life can be daunting, burning you out before you've even had a chance to shine. What do you do? In my case, I got caught in the act that I was using to hide behind. I was fortunate that my future husband was perceptive enough to see through my facade. It allowed me to realize that we fish out of water need help; and who better to write a guidebook than someone who has been a fish out of water her entire life?

Humorist Erma Bombeck wrote a book titled *If Life Is a Bowl of Cherries, What Am I Doing in the Pits?* Funny as that is, it inadvertently highlights a truism about life: It's all about perception. You might ask, "I'm a fish out of water. What's the good in that?" Well, it's a matter of perception. You either believe you're "in the pits," or you realize you're at the intersection of discovery and opportunity. How you come to understand that being a fish out of water is the best thing that could have ever happened to you is what this book is all about. And it may mean shifting your perception so that you absolutely *know* you've been dealt the best cards life has to offer.

Let's start with a description of what a fish out of water is. It literally refers to a living creature having been removed from the setting in which it's able to survive. So if you're a fish out of water, you've been taken out of your natural environment. You attract attention, usually because you're different from the people around you. You are perceived as someone who doesn't fit in; you're outside the norm, you think and dress differently; some may feel that you're too controversial. Many times, you're considered ahead of your time, maybe even an iconoclast. Whatever you are, you don't run with the pack; instead, you march to the beat of your own drum.

If I've just described you, count your blessings. You are indeed fortunate. Your natural characteristics are what will—and likely, already have—set you apart in a positive way. You may not feel very positive about those differences right now because you've been busy trying to wish them away or cover them up. The truth is, you will stand out not because you're different, but because you're solidly grounded in who you are—with no apologies. People will gravitate toward you because of your energy, confidence, and flair. But before any of that happens, you need to come to terms with being a fish out of water—and a Fearless Fish, at that!

I had to come to terms with being raised by a single father. I longed to have a mother like the other kids in my school. I wished for our family to have more money like my wealthier classmates, all of whom seemed to receive a credit card the day they became a bar or bat mitzvah. When I moved from Ohio to Alabama for college, I was not only seen as a Yankee, but I ran into prejudice as a Jew—one of 150 in a student body of 10,000. There, I came to realize that my differences sparked curiosity and, as a result, created opportunity. I had to come to terms with the fact that there were things about myself that I could change and others I was simply going to have to accept.

Being a Fearless Fish means *not* doing any of the following: hiding who you are; compromising your personality just to fit in; short-circuiting opportunities because you're afraid of what others will think; overemphasizing characteristics so others will think you're in the groove and on target; or letting others tell you how to think, feel, and act—just so that they'll feel comfortable and safe.

If there is one thing I've learned, it's that acting out of fear and living according to other people's needs will definitely pigeonhole you into being someone you're not; and that's not what life is about. The universe offers a myriad of ways in which we can express ourselves and find success on so many levels, both personal and professional. Our job is to be open to those possibilities and see how far we can go. Life truly is a journey; so why not make the most of it?

So, let's begin the journey of celebrating your distinctiveness. From my own personal experience of being a fish out of water, I've put together a series of steps to help you realize your full potential as a unique individual. They are:

Step 1: Go Fishing for the Real You

Step 2: Use Your Differences as a Lure

Step 3: Find a Few Fish Like You

Step 4: Swim in Their Ocean Your Way

Step 5: Put Yourself Out on the Line

Step 6: Evolve by Casting a Wide Net

Step 7: Reel in Your Unique Power

Step 1 to becoming a Fearless Fish out of water is to peel away the layers you've piled on in your attempts to fit in, uncovering the power of your authenticity. Shedding old habits is often essential to opening up to your authentic self. It's about being comfortable in your own skin and accepting yourself. Easier said than done, I know! It takes real courage to dispel the myths about you and find out how to be yourself honestly. *This* is fearlessness.

As CEO and chief creative officer of Big Fish Marketing, one of the entertainment industry's preeminent brand marketing and digital advertising agencies, I lead as a woman in a highly competitive, male-dominated field. I started my own ad agency at the age of 30 and 15 years later, I was named one of the top 10 digital advertising strategists in the country. My client list includes some of the most high-profile brands in the world: dozens of television networks, several motion picture studios, and even a hot cosmetics company. Having this kind of presence in the business world takes talent, but it also takes confidence and confidence didn't come naturally to this fish out of water.

Getting to know ourselves is a lifelong process.

Getting to know ourselves is a lifelong process. One of my closest friends recently said to me, "What if I've come this far and I still don't know who I am?" As much as we want to quickly understand ourselves, there are no shortcuts to the truth. We're deep and multifaceted, and we're changing all the time. But at our core—in our souls—we are stable, vibrant beings with philosophies, values, and perspectives that travel with us throughout our lives.

Open up to your authentic self. Sounds scary, huh? "The *real* me?" Sometimes we're not quite sure who that is. When we're used to feeling distant from the group, we tend to submerge our true selves in an effort to be accepted. The real movers and shakers in this world live their lives with conviction; they never hide who they are. They accept that they were born different or landed in circumstances that make them different, and they embrace the opportunity to stand out from the pack. We all have that same opportunity.

A friend of mine and a true Fearless Fish, Monica Halpert is one of the most creative people I've ever known. She is an idea machine who's totally tapped into pop culture. It's exciting just to be around her and see what she's into. The trouble is employers always want her to be *more* than the one with the big ideas; they want Monica to mold herself into a marketing role where she has to pore over research, crunch numbers, manage staff, and write strategy. Her managers waste her innovative, multimillion-dollar mind with administrative duties rather than letting her flourish in a corner office as a tastemaker, thinking up one great concept after another and doing the stuff that *really* builds world-class brands. Monica has realized this and is repositioning herself as someone who could take on the role of chief creative officer—a relatively new title many companies are adding to their organizational charts. Being the first in a position that's essentially just been invented is the ideal next step for someone like Monica who likes to work on the cutting edge.

Nathalie Lubensky, senior vice president of Disney and ESPN Media Networks sees herself as a fish out of water. That strong outsider feeling came to her early on in life—so much so that being different has become second nature to her. No matter where she is, she knows she stands out and uses that to her advantage.

> *I've felt like a fish out of water for so long that it's now a natural state. There hasn't been a time when I've walked into a room and felt accepted. I have never had the acceptance my son does (he's biracial). I never fit in with African-Americans because I'm Haitian; my parents were prejudiced against them. It was all about class not color. Class and race issues follow me everywhere.*

Despite these class and race issues, Nathalie has gone on to hold a hugely impressive and demanding position. As a woman of color in a predominantly white, male environment, she is sensitive to the need for greater diversity among the staff; she knows what value diverse perspectives can give to a company. She puts her values into practice by being an agent for change, helping create a culture she can embrace, and by doing so, positively illuminates her differences.

It's time for you to close the book on other people's stories and ideas about who you are so that you can finally introduce yourself the way you want to be known. If you've been pigeonholed as rigid, break out and show that you're someone who shapes his or her environment to allow for a flow of fresh ideas. If you feel that no one really "gets you," stop worrying about it; accept yourself as being ahead of the curve. Your personal perspective about yourself is key to being a successful fish out of water.

Anybody can be fearless when things are going great. It's in times like these that you have to search yourself and be brutally honest. One of the reasons we sometimes feel that we don't fit in with others is because we actually don't like ourselves. Consider whether this might be your situation and think about *why*. It could be that you're judging yourself according to other people's standards. Did Eleanor Roosevelt hide herself because she was a strong, intelligent woman who understood people, business, and politics? No. She knew she had a voice and demanded that people listen, in spite of the fact that she was operating in arenas largely considered to be "men's territory." She famously once said, "No one can make you feel inferior without your consent." Did Wilma Rudolph decide to remain in the shadows just because she had polio? No. She became a basketball star in high school, and then she became the first American woman to win three gold medals in track in the 1960 Summer Olympics in Rome.

Eleanor was immediately categorized by others as an outsider trying to break into a man's world, while Wilma was ostracized for her disability and for being an African-American woman. But neither one let these obstacles stop them from doing amazing things. Both women used their innate talents and personalities, as well as their obvious differences from those around them, to overcome personal and public challenges.

As a fish out of water, do you feel that part of your life is based on other people's assumptions of who *they* think you should be? Do you internalize their opinions and try to meet their expectations? Are you living your life for them instead of you? If so, then it's time to bust out and time for you to be yourself—*all* the time.

Many people who want the world to be safe and comfortable might wish that you would look, act, and think just like them. And as much as they don't want you to be distinctive, they don't want to be seen as different either. So they hide behind masks, afraid that the world might one day find them out. That behavior is based on fear of the unknown, of what is different, of what isn't immediately understood, and of being judged by others.

To live your life in fear is essentially not to live.

Then there are the times when you *know* you aren't being the real you. This, too, damages your relationships in the long term; how can someone truly know you if you aren't being authentic? You can probably remember moments when you caught yourself wondering why you were acting or saying things that felt unnatural. You immediately knew that you were not being yourself. What do you do when this is happening?

The phrases "get real" and "reality check" both apply at a time like this. Think about how you dishonor or disrespect yourself, the other person, or your organization when you're not authentic.

The best relationships are based on honesty. The best relationship you can have with yourself is one where you acknowledge every part of yourself, understanding both the good and bad.

Graciela Meibar, VP of global sales training and global diversity at Mattel, knows this firsthand: "You have to be authentic. You will always have to accommodate the overall culture to some degree, but never stop being who you are," she says. "If we are not true to who we are, or we pretend or please, we lose who we are."

> *As a woman, as a Latina, I have to establish myself by the way I dress and how I express myself. I look professional, but with style, which is authentic to who I am and very different from other women in the company. I like to stand out. I'm a good storyteller, using stories from the past to make points so I don't sound like fluff. I am unique, and I don't want to blend in.*

Free yourself from the desire to conform. Fish out of water are nonconformists. They are the rule breakers simply because they don't fit in with the norm. They know—like Patagonia's founder Yvon Chouinard—that you can't compromise your values to fit in. Chouinard has said, "Everybody tells me it's an undervalued company, that we could grow this business like crazy and then go public, make a killing. But that would be the end of everything I've wanted to do. It would destroy everything I believe in."

Authenticity means saying what you do and doing what you say. It's about being genuine.

As Chouinard illustrates, authenticity means being genuine. You aren't a chameleon changing with the scenery, or an actor slipping in and out of costume. You're an individual with a wealth of ideas, skills, and talents. It's up to you to show what you can do with them. It can be frustrating and lonely to think or look differently from everyone; but when you give the best representation of who you are from your core, you can really shine.

Reshaping or hiding who you are will not only provoke negative impressions of you; it will cheapen your own experience. I see so many businesswomen trying to underplay their femininity because in their minds, becoming less of a woman is the only way to be taken seriously in the corporate world. I just don't buy it. Being a stunner with a sharp mind is an unbeatable combination.

Playing down your best assets so that others will feel comfortable around you isn't real, it's self-absorbed. I'm a very feminine woman who sits at the table with some of the most powerful men in business. I don't try to be cute, and I don't try to win them over with sex appeal. They pay attention to me because I'm professional, directed, self-assured, and have ideas that are appropriate to the project.

Timing is essential with emotion and its expression.

Timing is essential with emotion and its expression. Not everything has to be expressed the moment it's occurring. Balancing your intellect with your emotions is key in business. Years ago, I had a client who was like a human chainsaw. Everything that came out of her mouth was cruel and insensitive. She said something once during a meeting that struck me hard, and I felt myself choke up. Knowing that my tears would only escalate the tension in the room and prevent the outcome we needed, I controlled my emotions and excused myself. After a short break, I calmed down and returned to the meeting only to sit down to the kindest words I'd ever heard her say. She wanted to know if everything was okay. I assured her that I was fine; and she was pleasant for the rest of the meeting. I had disarmed her by maintaining my dignity. It was about holding my own and not letting someone else break me. Containment, when it is needed, can be the most powerful expression of your authenticity.

You may think that showing your emotion *is* being authentic. As I said earlier, though, being emotional in front of others can be perceived as manipulative and weak. Many times, an emotional outburst will change the workplace dynamic. Coworkers will often decide, unconsciously, that you see yourself as the victim or a martyr. Such a label causes you to lose your personal power and makes your coworkers feel that they need to take care of you. You've established a dependent/codependent relationship dynamic—a very dangerous scenario for a fish out of water. Just like a betrayal of trust in a romantic relationship, it's an uphill battle to put things right after that.

Let's talk about an important subject: passion and emotions. Some people might describe "being emotional" as simply showing how passionate you are about your job or another specific subject. I see a difference between *having* passion and *being* passionate. In corporate America, having passion means that you're dedicated to seeing something be successful, understood, and recognized for what it truly is. Having passion for something is attractive; people will gravitate to you, and they'll become energized and engaged with you. However, *being* passionate may very well have the opposite effect on coworkers. They may decide that you're emotionally out of control and unbalanced. They'll be focused on your behavior rather than on what you have to say.

To avoid this, it's important to unearth your passion, and move in a direction that resonates with your soul. If you love what you do, the work and money will come, as will happiness. We often choose a course such as finance, law, or the family business because our parents want us to, or our friends have, or because it just seems like the right thing to do. But what if that's not where your passion lies? You'll end up in a career that doesn't fit, especially if you're a creative type. So what do you do to get off the track you're on? If you've been on a specific career track for some time, this will most likely seem an impossible move and fear is going to get a grip on you.

Not to worry—completely turning your life inside out is not what's being asked of you. Instead, you need to explore how you can take your skill sets and your passion for something and combine them. Let's say you've been an actuary for years. Outside of work, you love animals. Why not be CFO for a zoo or a business manager for a pet retailer, or put your talents to work at a bird sanctuary? If you've been a lawyer, but are drawn to cases that advocate for children, how about becoming a family law mediator? The idea is to take your skills and see where in the *overall* industry you can fit.

My father, for example, sold advertising for radio stations and newspapers and for a short time had his own ad agency. He was fantastic at it, but he eventually wanted to slow down and do something for the greater good. He now substitute teaches, sharing his accrued life experience with middle school and high school students. He is living proof that we can all wear many different hats and have several careers, if we have the courage to change direction.

We can wear many different hats and have several careers during our lifetime.

News flash: You must find a place to work that suits your personality. Though you may initially disagree with this statement, it's something to really think about. Life is not just about survival; it's about thriving. Where you live and work has a lot to do with how happy you're going to be in life. Consider your location. Are there places that are more aligned with your chosen field, your interests, your personality? If the location needs to change, then make it happen.

No matter where you are, if you are authentic, people will automatically open up to you. You will engage people. When I moved to Los Angeles from Atlanta I was seeking to make my dreams come true. Fortunately, so were all the people I met. L.A. is a city of dreamers and dream makers. By revealing what I wanted, I connected with people. Now I live in Santa Fe, New Mexico, because I'm seeking balance and enlightenment. In Santa Fe, the people I meet are very real and deep; they connect from the heart and engage the mind. I can sit and converse with people, disagree with them, and still be liked for who I am. I can simply be myself.

No matter what environment you are in or how carefully designed your life may be, challenges will occur. When your best-laid plans fall through or you make a grand mistake, you need to set aside your emotions, take responsibility, state how you're going to resolve the issue, and then offer options for resolution. You're going to make mistakes at some point; it's inevitable. The best option is to be mature in your response, take your punches—this is business, after all—and learn from the experience so that you can move forward in a positive manner.

Getting the place where you live right is one thing; learning how to interact with the people there is another. All relationships are charged by one or more emotions. One of the trickiest relationship dynamics to navigate is when you hire or work closely with a friend or family member as either an employee or partner. This scenario is ripe for abuses of all kinds, and emotions come easily into play. I can speak to this from experience since my husband is my business partner, my sister handles creative work for us, and I've had two of my closest friends work for the agency. Essentially, it's about remaining professional, setting boundaries as to what is appropriate and what isn't, and being respectful of each other.

When you're a fish out of water, the norm isn't going to be normal for you. So everything we've covered up to this point will require greater attention on your part than it might for your peers; all the more reason to spend time finding your passion, determining where you fit best in the workplace and in your current job, and being authentic.

Make a great first impression. Over the years I've become close to several people who, for better or worse, make a great second impression. They like to shock others and amuse themselves by pushing the envelope when they meet someone for the first time. It's kind of like saying, "Hey this is absolutely the *most* hideous I can be. If you can take it, we can be friends." Obviously, I'm someone who gravitates to people who are different, and I'm not put off easily.

Most of the world, though, lives in fear of being embarrassed. So it's important to show yourself honestly the first time, then gradually let people see all of you once they've earned that privilege. To start, share what you have going for you instead of talking about what you're missing. There's no need to blurt out your list of wounds because you think that revealing them will somehow make others understand you. True alliances cannot be formed by manipulation or by using sympathy. Choose what to bring forward in a way that celebrates who you are and not in a way that's designed to pull heartstrings. Oprah didn't get where she is by complaining, as she could rightfully have done, that she didn't have good role models—instead, she became one.

Choose what to bring forward in a way that celebrates who you are and not in a way that's designed to pull heartstrings.

Here's a personal example of someone who made a behavioral choice that went south and changed my impression of her forever.

I hired a young lady who had a pedigree resume and who literally looked the part of a marketing coordinator. She was articulate, had great schooling, and terrific job experience. The position was difficult on many levels with lots of stress. Her experience showed that she would be perfect for the position. My mistake was in not calling her previous employer.

After two months, I noticed that she wasn't getting the job done. I brought her into my office to discuss my observation. She immediately started crying—like a faucet turned on. This went on for 30 minutes. I've never seen so much water come out of a person. Seeing her distress, I shifted into caretaker mode instead of keeping the meeting on a professional basis. Well, I left the room so the young woman could collect herself, but was feeling at a loss with how to deal with her.

While she was in my office, I called my business coach. She suggested that the woman needed to go home and determine if this was the right job for her. I didn't follow her advice.

Days later, I got a call from a client complaining about the young woman not having handled something appropriately. I went to talk to her, but she wasn't at her desk. I searched her desk to find the client's materials so I could resolve the issue. Her desk was in shambles; nothing was organized. I couldn't find what I needed, which really hampered my ability to work with the upset client.

The first chance I could, I called her into my office to confront her with the client's distress and what I'd discovered. It was déjà vu. The young woman did an exact repeat of our last meeting—30 minutes of crying, this time stating that her father had cancer and that she couldn't do the work assigned her. I told her to go home and decide if this was the right job for her. She went home . . . and I never heard from her again.

I called her former employer, and guess what he said? "She's a crier."

Contrast the previous story with that of Erica Huggins, senior executive VP of Imagine Entertainment, who always knew she would succeed. Her mother was a huge proponent of the idea that "You can do anything," and her father would give her validation for things she did that were outside the box. He would say about his daughter, "You can drop Erica anywhere in the world and she can find her way back." A true Fearless Fish out of water, Erica quickly learned to feel comfortable making decisions that were right for her, not someone else.

You have to choose the path that suits you, unlike so many people who go down the programmed path.

I felt like a fish out of water in high school in Los Angeles. When I was a sophomore, I was sent to the

Stanford summer program in theater, after which I was expected to go back to my high school life. I realized this wasn't working; I wasn't fitting in with the girls and all the high school stuff. I couldn't be part of the group; and I had to make choices that were right for me.

I ended up going to Hampshire College, a small, alternative college in Amherst, Massachusetts. That was considered weird, not a normal choice for a kid from the Valley. Hampshire had no grades, all mentoring. Not at all like UCLA, where all my friends were going.

My dad was a professor and there was a lot of academia around me. I wanted to be away from my folks to be who I was going to become. I felt like an alien in L.A.

It was a great feeling being at Hampshire College. I felt like I was a part of something. The school attracted a lot of creative, out-of-the-box thinkers—like the guy who created Ultimate Frisbee. I spent every summer in New York and traveled abroad a lot back then. I had started making documentary films when I was in college, so in order to make money while doing that, I moved back to L.A. to apprentice as a film editor at Cannon Films. My boss was an old, drunk film editor. I turned that situation to my benefit and learned how to do what he was supposed to do—my boss's job! It was fun and I felt really good inside.

In trying situations, there were doubtlessly times when Erica wanted to be a crier; but she wasn't. Instead, she took bold steps and made choices that were initially frightening but ultimately rewarding. The bottom line is, tears have no place in the office. Yes, sadness or frustration may be authentic, but the expression of these feelings can have a manipulative effect, and manipulation does not lead to authenticity. Tears can often influence a response;

they beg for sympathy, and that's not appropriate or helpful in a business environment.

Erica's experience is a testament to the fact that it's best to know your boundaries, and take responsibility for your reality and your choices. Be aware of the behaviors you use to stand out. Some women may use crying to manipulate and some men can allow their tempers to flash or turn an argument around to deflect blame. You can break these stereotypes by understanding who you are and what it means to just be you, without using your emotions to shock and force people to see you. Otherwise, all you're doing is using a defense mechanism to define who you are.

Revealing yourself involves making careful choices and having patience. It's like peeling and eating an artichoke. Peel one leaf at a time; don't shed all your leaves at once and reveal your tender heart before your relationships have a solid foundation. There is a lot of good taste in the smaller bits along the way.

Bust the myths about you. Let's face it: You're branded the day you walk in the door. Conclusions are instantly drawn about you, myths based on assumption and impression. Any of those myths could be negative. Instead of standing back and pointing fingers— and carrying a chip on your shoulder, which encourages exclusion—change perceptions of you by fearlessly showing yourself. Bust the myths.

Change perceptions of you by fearlessly showing yourself.

Andy Warhol did that by boldly being himself as have many other artists and industry leaders. Warhol was one of the first major American artists to be open about his homosexuality; and he was criticized for it. He wrote in his book *Popism*, "I decided I just wasn't going to care, because those were all the things that I didn't want to change anyway, that I didn't think I 'should' want to change. . . . Other people could change their attitudes, but not me." And lo and behold—people *did* change their attitudes.

I had a similar experience while attending the University of Alabama. I found myself confronted by a lot of people who didn't know anyone Jewish, or who had a negative impression of Jews because of prejudice they'd learned at home. In my four years there, I worked to dispel the myths about myself and others like me by joining the Jewish sorority and developing its presence on campus in a way that had never been done before.

Greg Clark, affiliate marketing manager at Comedy Central and Spike, is another myth-buster. At 25 years of age, he's the youngest member of a nearly all-female staff. Instead of acting like the young guy hotshot, he broke the stereotype by being disciplined about his work and agreeable to his superiors. He knew he needed to listen and learn and not come in acting like a know-it-all. And his attitude is opening minds and doors.

> *When I came into MTV Networks, most people working here were women. I asked them, 'Why me?' They said, 'To bring in someone different.' But I was a young white man. I've learned more about women through this experience; there is a man's world and a woman's world. In a man's world, men say how things are. Women, on the other hand, take feelings into account—there's more compassion. That's the culture. They make the worker feel wanted. So we feel accepted. No matter what our gender or skin color.*
>
> *My hurdle is that I'm in my mid-20s, and I can be goofy. But in the end, I mean business. I just use humor to*

> *defuse the situation. What people don't get about me is that I really am serious. I show them by dressing up and making presentations at staff meetings in a professional manner. It throws people off, and lets me be seen for my talents.*

When attorney Kim Deck started out at JAMS—the largest mediation firm in the country—she was up against a lot of resistance; both because she was a woman in a man's field and because her father was the chairman. To prove it was her talent and skill and not nepotism that got her where she was, Kim worked harder than anyone else in the firm to make things happen. Everyone benefited. Recently, Kim was voted one of the Top 40 Mediators by the California Bar Association.

> *At the beginning of my career, I felt like a fish out of water. When I was starting out in my early 30s, I was competing with retired judges for cases. I was one of the few lawyer mediators and one of the only female mediators in California.*
>
> *I had a mentor say to me, "If you want to be something, say you are that—you have to embody what you say." I just said, "I'm a mediator," and reinvented myself.*
>
> *I use being a woman to my advantage; most of my clients are men. I've always gotten along with men and have a lot of fun with them. I play up my great sense of humor and my warmth. Warmth, understanding, and compassion get the deals done. I'm dogged in my commitment to helping people. I do everything humanly possible to make things happen. The stakes are high—*

> *it's a lawsuit, so it's serious business. It takes analysis, great listening skills, and a memory for facts.*
>
> *To dispel any myths around being a female mediator and a lawyer, I really sold the fact that I was the kind of person clients could relate to. They were mostly young women, so I played that to my advantage and it was a game changer.*
>
> *When I was a kid, I had to change schools every year. I guess that's why I'm actually comfortable with trail blazing.*

To blaze your own trail, it's important to bust any negative myths about you. However, if those myths are positive, you may choose to play them up and create a mystique. During my career, I've known people whose great reputations were built on their past or pedigree. Whether you're an ex-jock, whiz kid, military man, or from a powerful family, playing up rather than playing down, what sets you apart can take you a long way on your road to success.

Apologize for who you are and others will see you as someone to pity.

Accept yourself and others will follow. Apologize for who you are and others will see you as someone to pity. Saying you're sorry for your imperfections puts doubt in people's minds about your value. Schoolmasters worried about young Albert Einstein—he wasn't like the other kids. He felt out of place growing up, victimized by an educational system that stifled originality and creativity. He didn't begin speaking until he was three years old. He didn't fit in with his classmates and, because of what looked like learning difficulties, there was some talk that he was retarded. The headmaster at one of Einstein's schools told him that he would never be a successful professional and recommended he attend trade school. A teacher told him he wouldn't amount to anything.

When you're different from the norm, you already attract attention; but the good news is that attracting attention may be the best thing that ever happened to you. Einstein followed his path, and the world paid attention. The same is true for everyone who lives their truth with conviction.

When you're different from the norm, you already attract attention. The good news is that attracting attention may be the best thing that ever happened to you.

I think the people who are fish out of water are the ones to admire. Imagine what would have happened if Tiger Woods' father hadn't dared put his child prodigy in the limelight or encouraged a record-breaking career in golf because Tiger is multiracial and most professional golfers are white. Woods is gifted, he performs brilliantly, and he's an inspiration to golfers and non-golfers everywhere.

Feeling that you're a fish out of water can happen anywhere in any type of business. Jason Heller, former managing director of Horizon Interactive, started out in the hip-hop industry and now circulates throughout the corporate world with his own Internet-based business. When Jason was in the hip-hop world, he hung out with graffiti artists and break-dancers, even though he had grown up in a stable middle class home, not the projects. For him, if life is a circle, he would be standing with one foot in and one foot out.

I was a white kid born and raised in the Bronx. I started in the hip-hop industry as a DJ at age 16 in the New York City nightlife scene. It was exhilarating. I've always felt like I was different from other people. I have little tolerance for mediocrity.

At age 18, I ended up dropping out of college. It seemed like a waste of time. I butted heads with teachers who never had any real-world experience. I wasn't about theory, I was about practice. So, I went full time into the music business. I felt like I was accomplishing something with my life by working.

My first record was recorded in the early '90s, and it was a huge success. My partner was DJ Shok, who has sold 20 million records to date. The New York City underground sound was our thing.

In 1995, I used the advent of the Internet to create a web site and started infiltrating chat rooms, pushing our artists. We started a grassroots marketing firm trying to promote our artists—putting stickers everywhere. My record company was called Mass Vinyl Recordings. I had a No. 2 Maxi Billboard Single for an artist of mine called Hi Tech.

I left the music business with a thirst for the Internet, and I went to work for a traditional direct marketing company to help them establish an Internet marketing division. My partner, Jason Burnam, and I knew we'd start our own agency shortly thereafter. Eight months later, in 1998, we left to start Mass Transit out of a three-bedroom apartment in Brooklyn. I translated what I had learned as an independent record company producer into cheap guerrilla marketing. We found clever ways to get the word out for companies like Bertelsmann and Doubleday Direct Book Clubs.

> *Now I'm a hip-hop kid from the Bronx in a corporate world. I'm more successful than most MBA-educated types, and I have more fun. It has been both liberating and uncomfortable, because people in corporations are not like me.*

Heller is a prime example of why it's vital for you to embrace yourself as you are; to understand that the universe is ready to support those who accept themselves, pursue their passions, and contribute to the greater good. It knows that diversity is essential, and it doesn't need everyone to be alike. There are scores of successful fish out of water who have found alignment with that spiritual truth as they uncovered the meaning of self-acceptance and lived it fearlessly. They have also made an important determination in figuring out whether the company or organization they're in is a good fit.

Sometimes, you or those who have hired you really, *really* want the job to work out. But there are times when no amount of effort on either of your parts is going to help. Being a fish out of water is just something that can't be contained, retrofitted, suppressed, or managed in a way that is workable. When you need to soar, break out, or be the original thinker, then that's the only thing that will work. Not every company or organization can handle that; and that's when you need to channel your energies elsewhere. The clearer your perception of yourself is, the more readily that job will appear.

A great example of this—from a world where being a fish out of water is actually commonplace—is dancer and choreographer Twyla Tharp. Twyla became a superstar in the dance and film world, first with her own groundbreaking company and then as a choreographer for many major dance companies in the world. She's created more than 125 dances; choreographed five

Hollywood movies; directed and choreographed two Broadway shows; written two books; and received one Tony Award, two Emmy Awards, 17 honorary doctorates, the Vietnam Veterans of America President's Award, and the 2004 National Medal of the Arts.

Twyla, from a Quaker background, is described as being brash, uncompromising, unwilling to submit to authority, highly intellectual, totally lacking in humor, and defensive to a fault. Ballet was too restrictive, and modern dance was still somewhat claustrophobic. After a stint with the Paul Taylor Dance Company, she struck out on her own. Critics weren't sure what they were looking at when Twyla's routines first arrived on the dance scene; but her perseverance and passion over the years overcame critical scrutiny, and her vision as a choreographer has now become legendary. She says, "They called it vision; I call it analyzing what my strengths were. It just so happened there was no market whatsoever for my strengths."

Twyla continues to question and explore, and her trajectory through the heavens of life and dance remains bright as ever. She truly dances to her own drumbeat, having accepted her difference as the base structure from which she carves her future.

The key to developing self-acceptance is acknowledging what is in place, what is working—*having gratitude.*

The key to developing self-acceptance is acknowledging what is in place, what is working, and *having gratitude* for that. It's about turning your focus toward what you have instead of harboring a sense of scarcity and always focusing on what seems to be missing. When you live with the constant feeling that you don't have enough, you'll be seen that way, too; and you'll cultivate more of it. It's not attractive to others, and it doesn't attract more of anything to you except more scarcity. (A good way to attract scarcity is to walk around thinking, "But I'm so different from everyone. I just don't fit in.")

There's usually a gem inside even the most difficult of experiences.

You may say, "But it's been so hard! My glass is more empty than full." But I'm suggesting that you take a closer look and review those hard lessons with an eye toward the good they've given. There's usually a gem inside even the most difficult of experiences. I woke up to this realization a few years ago, after spending most of my life bemoaning that I'd moved seven times between the ages of three and six. What a shift came when I recognized what I'd gained from that early rootlessness. I've grown into a flexible, spontaneous, adaptable, and resourceful person who is unafraid of change, all valuable attributes in navigating the adult world. The glass is fuller than I once thought.

Gratitude is essential when you're a fish out of water.

Gratitude is essential when you're a fish out of water. Asked once if she had a good luck charm, comedienne Ellen DeGeneres said her good luck charm was her gratitude. Entertain gratitude, review the gifts of your life—including the diamonds in the rough—and list them. Then, keep this list handy. Refer to it. Add to it. Read it over every night before you go to bed or first thing when you wake up in the morning. It's easy to incorporate into a morning or evening routine. I occasionally ask others close to me—my daughter, my husband, my staff—what's making them happy, what they are satisfied with, what they are grateful for. Listening to their answers adds to my feeling of gratefulness.

Having gratitude keeps the focus on the half-full glass. And from that place of feeling fulfilled in your work and personal relationships, more fullness comes. As a fish out of water, you can lead with this sense of fullness. Before long, others will want to join you so they learn how to fill their glass. Where you once felt scarcity outside the circle, you will feel rewarded right where you are.

Gratitude also allows you to see where you currently are. I've noticed that a lot of young people just coming into the workforce arrive with some unrealistic expectations. Never having spent 40 hours a week in a closed work environment before, they don't always want to accept that corporate culture is not exactly like one's family scenario; though relationship dynamics often do come into play. In the business world, you have to learn to make your own way; something that can take time, depending on a number of variables. I've watch many of my clients put their bosses in parental roles and look for approval and handouts. A complaint I often hear is: "I've been in this position for years. I should have been promoted by now."

News flash: Management's timetable for advancement and your timetable are two different things. In a tough economy, it's going to be more difficult to advance, and you will be required to be more present, productive and inventive. It's not only about doing your job to the best of your ability, as stated in your job description; it's also a time for you to discover where you fit best in the organization considering your interests, skill sets, and ambitions. First, as we covered earlier, you need to determine if the company you're working with is a good fit. Second, you need to take into account the other employees, the direction the company is going, your focus versus the company's focus, and whether you have the experience that says you're ready for advancement. I know a guy named David who worked as an airport shuttle driver for a company in San Diego. He got up at 1 A.M. every morning, got to work by 3 A.M., and was on the road picking up his first passengers by 4 A.M. The crew he worked with covered the gamut of men and women from varying backgrounds. Most of them were, as he put it, "Pigpens"— sloppy folks who wore whatever they were eating and handled their clients like sheep. Many were obsessed with how much they made each day in tips. David is a 180-degree turn from these people.

The shuttle company has a limousine division, something you can apply to join after you've been driving airport shuttles for at least six months. You apply, your driving record with the company and client comments are reviewed, and you're either asked to join or not.

I was asked to join the limousine division after driving shuttles for three months—and I hadn't even applied. I was so grateful for having a job in the first place that I'd always dressed impeccably and looked just as together when I finished my day 10 to 12 hours later as when I'd arrived at work at 3 A.M. My attitude was that I was transporting people who deserved the utmost respect and consideration. I watched my language and was sensitive to my guests' needs.

Looking back on that period, I don't know how I got up at 1 A.M. and did that job for three months; but my gratitude and integrity was apparent to the powers that be. Not only was I asked to become a limo driver for them, I was asked to develop two training courses: one for the shuttle drivers and one for the reservations department. That was total icing on the cake. And the tips driving the limos were incredible!

Gratitude is a key virtue to cultivate. As David discusses in his story, integrity and respect are two others that go a long way in your relationship with yourself and with others. Another virtue that works well in all facets of business is a creative imagination. Creativity is what keeps everything evolving and interesting. Nothing works like a new idea to open minds and hearts and instigate more new ideas. Those with whom you work will immediately recognize all of these virtues, as they are integral components of the package we've covered: authenticity.

One more important business virtue is managing your perceptions and expectations. Let both get out of hand and you'll find you're a fish out of water swimming not only against the current but up a waterfall. We all want to be successful at what we do, and we all want recognition for our accomplishments. If you focus on doing the work at hand to the best of your ability—and go beyond what's expected—then you'll get noticed. If your focus is simply on climbing the corporate ladder and attaining kudos, then you'll begin missing important details and your work relationships will begin to reflect your lack of authenticity. Accept the person that you are and manage your expectations. Otherwise, you're in for disappointment and a work situation that is less fulfilling and enjoyable.

Key business virtues to cultivate: integrity, respect, creative imagination, managing your perceptions and expectations.

News flash: Coworkers see right through people who aren't being authentic. That's why the first step in coming to terms with being a fish out of water is dissolving the layers you've piled on trying to fit in and discovering the power in your authenticity.

This life takes courage. It takes courage simply to show up every day when you're a fish out of water. You can be proud of that. Courage comes from confidence, and confidence comes from believing in your worthiness. And developing that sense of worthiness begins by actively practicing belief in yourself (I'll go more deeply into ways of practicing belief in Step 7). To begin, look at your track record—all the times you got it right—and then recite an affirmation several times a day, using words that describe you like someone who loves you dearly would. Try on "I'm talented"/"I'm inspiring"/"I'm creative." It helps to hear it, because when you believe in yourself, others will, too.

We've covered a lot of material, so now it's time for you to do some work that will really help you to identify your unique gifts. By the time you complete this book, the exercises you'll find at the end of each step will have helped you come to terms with and capitalize on being a fish out of water. This step involved opening up to your authentic self, letting go of the need to conform, busting myths about yourself, figuring out how to make a great first impression, and learning to accept yourself. You are definitely on your way. Step 2, "Use Your Differences as a Lure," will show you how to go about capitalizing on your uniqueness.

Step 1 Exercises

Because you are a fish out of water, your path has not always been easy.

List one big challenge you've encountered.

_____

_____

_____

Is there anything positive that came out of that challenge?

_____

_____

_____

Describe what is unique about you.

_____

_____

Do you look different from others? How?

_____

_____

_____

Do you think differently than others? How?

_____

_____

_____

Do you act differently than others? How?

_____

_____

_____

What do you wish others would accept about you that you simply cannot change or do not want to change?

_____

_____

_____

List why you feel that these unique qualities are advantages to your company and/or industry.

1. _____
2. _____
3. _____
4. _____
5. _____

How are you being pigeonholed? For example: You are thought of as rigid, quick tempered, too sweet, and so forth.

_____

_____

_____

How can you turn these perceptions about you into positive attributes?

_____

_____

_____

Create a daily mantra to quietly say to yourself that turns your unique qualities into a positive. For example: "I am talented, inspiring, and creative."

_____

_____

_____

Give gratitude every day. What are you thankful for in this moment?

_____

_____

What are you satisfied with in this moment?

_____

_____

Who can you thank for these blessings?

_____

_____

Step

Use Your Differences as a Lure

Fearless Fish Out of Water Know that What You Think Makes You Different

- Show the strengths of your differences.
- Never apologize for who you are.
- Celebrate your style.
- Compromise a little, keep a whole lot.
- Let others shine the light on you.
- Be an inspiration.

In grade school, my gym teacher spread out a colorful parachute on the floor of the basketball court. She asked the students to stand in a circle around it and tug the sides as hard as we could, then move our arms up and down until the parachute formed a big rainbow of waves. One by one, the other children did this, letting go of the edges and crawling underneath to experience being inside the circle of silk. Not me. I hung on tight and never left the edge. I knew I belonged outside the circle. And it's been that way all my life.

For years, I felt like the only odd one in the bunch, yet over time, I've come to know many others who feel like fish out of water. Whether they're the only woman on the board, the first person of color to hold their position, or the creative maverick in a large corporation, their stories prove that being noticeably different can draw people in and create tremendous opportunity.

I found my way "in" doing it my way.

As a business owner in the world of entertainment advertising, I created my success partly by giving up my desire to blend in with the pack, and instead—opting to amplify what makes me different. I found my way "in" by doing it my way.

I grew up—as most of us do—wanting to be like everyone else. I lived with my father and younger sister in a modest two-bedroom apartment in a Jewish suburb on Cleveland's east side. My mother was alive—something I told very few people—but she was ill and unfit to care for her children. In my world, I was the only kid who didn't have a mom, a two-story house, and her own car by the time she was 16. I was ashamed and certain that I was worth less than everyone else. Did my friends really like me? Deep down, I was sure they were faking it.

I would discover that the more I stood out, the more I became part of it all.

When it was time to apply for college, I chose the University of Alabama. My father could afford it, and I wouldn't know a soul. Perfect! No one would know my story, and I would finally fit in. Friends warned me that the Deep South was no place for someone like me, but I forged ahead, eager for the clean slate. I had no idea I'd learn some of the most important lessons of my life in my four years there. I would discover that the more I stood out, the more I became part of it all. I would learn everything that I needed to know about surviving as a creative thinker in corporate America. To this day, I draw on my experience at the University of Alabama to succeed in business—especially when I'm the only one like me in a room.

In August 1980, my father and I arrived in Birmingham on what had to be the most humid day in the state's *history. We rented a car to drive the hour south to Tusca-loosa, where I would start my freshman year at college. At a freeway off ramp, I noticed a big yellow sign tacked to a telephone poll that read, "KKK MEETING 8 P.M." A shiver ran up my spine, but I didn't say a word. There was no way we were turning back. We checked into our hotel and took a walk around campus, imagining what my new life would be like.*

My father had been a frat boy, and he urged me to go to rush the next morning and join a sorority. "It's a great way to make friends," he promised. I agreed to go.

The heat was relentless as I ventured bravely into the sun to find my new sisters. There they were—colorful clusters of girls gathered on Sorority Row. The cicadas droned, and over their constant, monotonous hum I could hear that familiar scolding voice in my head: Look at these girls! You don't fit in and you never will!

I ducked into some shade under a magnolia tree outside the Kappa Kappa Gamma house and sized up the competition: Makeup that had been skillfully applied earlier in the morning was showing wear; starched white monogrammed shirt collars were becoming damp; glossy hair neatly confined by fabric-covered headbands and bows was beginning to frizz; stockings were glued to legs by the humidity. What was I doing here? I was a girl who blasted Springsteen and Pink Floyd, who wore jeans so tight I had to lie down to zip them, and stood in line at midnight to see the Rocky Horror Picture Show. A prissy coed in Pappagallo I was not.

Just then, the doors to the antebellum mansion flung open and out filed dozens of exuberant girls chanting,

> *"Kappa Kappa Kappa Gamma! I'm so happy that I am a Kappa Kappa Kappa Gamma!"*
>
> *In moments, I was arm in arm with a sparkling Kappa in a baby blue cotton piqué shift. "Robin!" she sang gaily, glancing at my nametag, "I'm Kate." Then she noticed the word "Cleveland" under my name. "Why, Cleveland!" she cried. "Now, that's a long way from home. Is that Cleveland, Tennessee, or Cleveland, Mississippi?"*
>
> *"Ohio," I said, almost apologizing.*
>
> *"Well! A Yankee no less . . . girls, come here and meet the Yankee!"*

There I was—a fish out of water again. And this time, I was a bigger fish than ever. How would I ever make it here?

I decided to find what was familiar.

To start, I decided to find what was familiar. The Jewish sorority, Sigma Delta Tau, was small and unpopular—half the size of the other sororities—but I joined it. Right away, I discovered that my new sisters, as comforting and kind as they were, seemed outside of everything. They had no real presence on campus, rarely mixed with the other sororities, and they never socialized with gentile frat boys, only with the young Jewish men of Zeta Beta Tau. They did little to dispel the myths about Jews, and there were plenty of myths at a school with only 150 Jews in a student body of 10,000. Most students had never met anyone Jewish. I was astounded when a boy who grew up in Tuscaloosa took me on a date and started to pat the top of my head. When I asked him what he was doing he replied, "Daddy told me y'all have horns."

I remembered what my father had always said: "You're the director of your own movie. You get to be the leading lady, and you get to write the story line, you choose the location, cast, and crew." His words made sense now. I wanted to belong and I wanted to have more fun, and I could see that wasn't going to happen unless I did something differently. I decided to go out and invent the sorority I wanted.

The first step in doing so was sharing my vision of integrating the sorority fully into Greek life. At first, only a handful of my new sisters were interested. They were suspicious of this enthusiastic, slightly offbeat Yankee. But eventually, my persistence got them on board. With a sassy new pal from Miami Beach, I knocked on the doors of fraternity houses, asking to see the social chairman to set up mixers. Finally, one house reluctantly agreed to a "swap," and word quickly spread that we were a fun bunch, not a group to avoid.

We were shaking up the joint. But not all of my sisters liked the change. They weren't particularly religious, but they weren't comfortable socializing with the gentile boys. I can't say that I was either—I'd never known boys who wore pastel Ralph Lauren shirts, khakis, and penny loafers, who danced to beach music ("Be Young, Be Foolish, and Be Happy" was a favorite tune), hunted ducks and deer, and drank Wild Turkey from a silver flask. I was from a different universe. But I didn't let it stop me. I was looking for the great adventure and a chance to be the real me.

The next step was taking one of my own interests—music—and building on that to make a difference at the school. I leveraged the fact that I hailed from Cleveland, the rock and roll capital, and asked the Student Council to start a concert committee. I would be a leading member. They agreed and over the next few years, our organization, High Tide Productions, brought in top acts of the day—Stevie Nicks, Hall and Oates, the Go-Go's. I became well-known around campus, and when I graduated, I landed my first job with the largest music retailer in the Southeast, because of my involvement with High Tide.

By being different, I could attract what I wanted.

Throughout my next four years of college, in addition to my work with High Tide, I stayed involved in my sorority by serving as pledge class vice president, social chairman, and president of Sigma Delta Tau. The house doubled in size, and the sisters had a presence on campus and friends in every corner. By being different, I could attract what I wanted. Finally, I had found my way inside the circle.

Show the strengths of your differences. My experience at college marked one of the first times I understood the true importance of this statement. You can't be unforgettable unless you dare to be different. Graciela Meibar, whom I introduced in the first step, is another who might have missed her calling if she'd given in to social pressure. She was a Cuban immigrant fresh off the boat at 12 years of age, and she didn't know a word of English. As a young adult in the business world, her accent made it difficult for her to be accepted into the mainstream, but instead of disappearing into a job that didn't require excellent communications skills, she worked her way through the University of Southern California's school of international relations and struck up a relationship with a Cuban-American woman at Mattel who, several years later, helped her land a job in the company's Latin American division. "It wasn't about reinventing myself, but becoming one hundred percent me," she says.

When you stand out, you attract attention.

The United States prides itself on being a "melting pot"—a collection of different cultures coming together to form a united whole. To promote this, almost everywhere we go, uniformity, not individuality, is encouraged, in school, at work, and even in social settings. The culture relies on a tacit agreement by everyone to do things a certain way—and those who don't agree stand out. But you have to remember: *That* is exactly where the opportunity lies. When you stand out, you attract attention. From that position, you can find your unique way "in" and really make a difference.

At 27 years of age, I was manager of creative services at Turner Broadcasting in Atlanta. The next year, I was promoted to director of affiliate marketing for Turner Network Sales, serving TNT, TBS, Headline News, and CNN. I was highly visible; my voice was heard; I held a position of power. But I thought differently from everyone else, and I was outspoken.

The trouble was that I wanted to fit in, and to do that I thought I needed to be as much like my colleagues as I could. I was sure this was the route to respect and acceptance. Wasn't it better not to make waves? On my drive into the office, I would rehearse for the day's meetings. "I'm not going to say anything," I would promise myself. "I'm not going to argue, I'm not going to try to get my point across." In the meeting, all would be well until a colleague said something so inside the box I would forget everything and burst out with my thoughts. The others may not have thought like me, but they listened. And at the end of the day, it worked. Turner was one of my clients when I started my own company, and they're my client to this day.

I'm a fish out of water, and I wouldn't trade what I do for anything.

I knew I would stand out as a female ad agency owner. I knew that most agency owners were men, especially in the entertainment industry. But I had experience and determination, and owning an agency was my ticket out from under the glass ceiling. I had to do it. Fifteen years later, there are still very few female ad agency owners—and even fewer who run agencies focused on harnessing the power of the Internet. I'm a fish out of water, and I wouldn't trade what I do for anything.

Today, I "own" that I'm noticed partly because I stand out. It's unexpected to see a highly feminine woman with a powerful client list like mine walk into the room. I shine a light on my differences—I'm not the average agency owner—and I'm original in how I dress, wearing funky suits accessorized with heirloom or ethnic jewelry. When a client thinks, "I'm looking for something different," I send the message that I'm the one they're looking for.

Director of media and entertainment for Unilever USA, Babs Rangaiah is someone else who has attracted interest because he stands out and does so with distinction. He's an East Indian man creating campaigns for global personal care, home care, and food brands. People pay attention to this creative businessman who's become a sensation with innovative campaigns like Dove's Campaign for Real Beauty, which features a Self-Esteem Fund designed to educate and inspire girls about a wider definition of beauty.

Rangaiah's differences give him a refreshing perspective and people want to hear it. He puts people at ease with his humor ("I'm the other Babs," he likes to say, referring to Barbra Streisand), and keeps his great ideas out in front. When it comes to standards of beauty, Babs thinks differently, and he's taking everyone with him.

When you're a fish out of water, the best strategy is to give a fearless representation of who you are, to be genuine.

When you're a fish out of water, the best strategy is to give a fearless representation of who you are—to be genuine. This sincerity can be attractive; it shows trustworthiness, which has an appeal that can transcend stereotypes and win people over.

On the *Barbara Walters Special* following the 2007 Academy Awards, host Ellen DeGeneres talked about coming out on air a decade earlier. She said she was scared to death. "Why did you put yourself through that?" Barbara asked.

"It's about living your truth," said Ellen. "That's all it is."

"It's about living your truth."

Ellen could have packed it up and returned to the comedy club circuit when her show was cancelled after her daring, groundbreaking leap. Instead, with honesty, humor, and talent, she reached into America's heart. And heartland. *Los Angeles Times* staff writer Paul Brownsfield has called DeGeneres " . . . America's lesbian—a uniter." She believes in herself and is boldly genuine, and people all across the country—even in more conservative regions—appreciate that. Living her differences honestly is Ellen's way in.

Ellen is the queen of living by her truth and decisions. She's authentic. She tells the truth and she makes it funny. She's charismatic, warm, and witty, with appeal that spans a broad age range and demographic. She loves people and loves being in the limelight, and she's combined the two by creating community on camera. Ellen was voted "Favorite TV Host" in one of *Time* magazine's polls, beating out the likes of Oprah Winfrey, Regis Philbin, and Meredith Vieira. NBC calls her a beloved television icon and entertainment pioneer. American Express partnered with her for its ad campaign, "My Life, My Card." Her talk/variety show, *The Ellen DeGeneres Show*, won 15 Emmy awards in its first three seasons and has garnered many other industry awards. And the list of her achievements goes on.

Ellen returned to ABC in 2007 to host the Academy Awards, the network's biggest ratings platform of the year. Drawing attention to herself as the first openly gay host of the Oscars, in her opening remarks Ellen said, "Such diversity in the room in a year when there's been so many negative things said about people's race, religion, and sexual orientation! And I want to put this out there: If there weren't blacks, Jews, and gays, there would be no Oscars, or anyone named Oscar, when you think about that."

Ellen "puts it out there" and she does it without compromise. Instead of retreating when her TV career took a dive, she held true to herself and her values and became a star beyond her wildest dreams.

Who would have expected all of this from the comedienne-actress who took a huge career risk in 1997, coming out in character on her sitcom, *Ellen*. That episode received an Emmy, but ratings fell and ABC cancelled her show. A few hard years followed, but Ellen held to her truth and found her place again in the limelight when NBC took a chance on her with a daily talk/variety show. The rest, as they say . . .

How do you stand out? What are the advantages in it for you? For your organization? Do you lead the way with the strengths of your differences? If not, a good place to start is by recognizing your own truths, believing in what's possible, and never apologizing for who you are. It takes practice and a lot of guts. But look how far you've already come, stepping out from the norm, accepting that you don't blend in and knowing you belong exactly as you are.

Acceptance. That's what we have to do as fish out of water, not try to change ourselves as much as accept ourselves for who we are. Insanity happens when we don't accept what we can't change. For so long I tried to act like or be like other people that I admired instead of realizing that those people connected with me because of how unique I was. Being different was a big reason why I was in their lives.

Never apologize for who you are. When I graduated from the University of Alabama, I was a fish out of water and a happy one. What had changed in my years there was my view of myself. I finally accepted myself for who I am, and as I did, I discovered that others did, too. I offered something different, I did it without apology, and the effect was positive and lasting.

Fish out of water are often trailblazing individuals who accomplish big things in their unique way.

Fish out of water are often trailblazing individuals who accomplish big things in their unique way. They make their mark not by being like everyone else but by turning heads and being unforgettable.

One unforgettable Fearless Fish out of water is Kristina Song—currently VP of programming at Time-Warner—an Asian woman who is changing perceptions.

> *My family and I emigrated from Korea when I was three years old. I grew up in Downey, California, a suburb of Los Angeles. When we first moved into that town, they had just lifted the closed community ordinances, but no one was happy we were living there. My family endured dead rats thrown onto our driveway, birds shot down into our swimming pool, firecrackers put in our mailbox. I was regularly teased for my Asian eyes.*
>
> *Today, Downey is very racially mixed, but when I first moved there, I was a real fish out of water. After college, I*

moved from California to New York, where today I am head of programming at Time-Warner Cable. I have found comfort in a company where many of the departments are headed by women. One of those women is an old law school buddy of mine who is also Korean. Because of this, I don't feel as much of a fish out of water anymore. But it hasn't always been that way.

When I wanted to make the leap from lawyer to running a business unit at a major media company, it wasn't easy to convince higher-ups. There's a perception that Asians make good lawyers because they are diligent and hard working, but we are not seen as businesspeople because we are thought of as quiet and reserved rather than gregarious and creative.

My personality fits in with mainstream corporate culture. But, every time you change where you're working you have to prove yourself. But, I have an extra burden of being identified as Asian. I have to overdeliver to be seen the same. My father warned me that I would have to deal with the aftermath of the Korean War all my life. "To be considered the same, you're going to have to run faster, be smarter, be tougher than the rest." My brother-in-law, who is a fourth generation Chinese-American, is still asked, 'What country are you from?' He grew up in Savannah, Georgia, and is a doctor!

To change perceptions, I work against type. I throw people off with my openness and general friendliness. I'm extroverted, not the stereotypical shy Asian woman. It would have been easier to build my career as a lawyer and not have to prove myself in a new way, but using what's different about me to make the transition paid off, because I'm so happy now. Every day is invigorating.

You need to act like *you*.

Sometimes the renegade with the breakthrough ideas can be exactly what's needed to improve an organization; the one who makes people uncomfortable could be the agent for change. It doesn't mean you have to ruffle everyone's feathers to get somewhere in life. But you need to act like *you*.

Vinnie Malcolm, former vice president/general manager, KTLA-TV Los Angeles, didn't try to conceal or apologize for anything when he applied for a position at Tribune Broadcasting. He knew what he had to offer, he knew what he wanted, and he went after it. "At the time, everyone was looking for someone black. I wouldn't have gotten those opportunities without a diversity mandate. But that will only get you in the door; it won't keep you there." When Vinnie headed KTLA/The CW in Los Angeles, he was the only black general manager at Tribune Broadcasting, as well as the only person of color to head a business unit. "Others at Tribune didn't have the life experience or business skills I had," explains Vinnie. "So it was a good fit. Now people look at differences favorably."

Graciela Meibar, whom I've mentioned before, is another who blazed trails by boldly being herself and being exceptional as VP of global sales training and global diversity at Mattel.

When I first arrived in the U.S. in 1970 from Cuba, it was a new world, a new culture. We were in Miami first and five days later, we were in L.A. with my Dad's cousin. I spoke no English and went from living in the country to living in the city. I had no friends. I left everybody I knew behind. I was excited and full of fear and, at times, very lonely.

I didn't have it easy when I entered the workforce, but I didn't back down. My first job out of college was at an aerospace company that sold aluminum and titanium products. After being there for six months, I was promoted into customer service, where there were only guys—all engineers. A few would make fun of my accent. One customer complained that he couldn't understand me. I couldn't understand him, either, because he had a heavy southern accent.

One day, I was leaning against the door in my boss's office and an engineer pinched me in the middle of my back. I slapped him. My boss pulled me aside and said, 'Are you okay? You want to talk to anyone?' I said, 'This issue is under control.' I had to set boundaries.

I stood out from the others, but I set myself apart even more: I made it my business to learn more about what went on at the company. I asked engineers to explain things to me. I'd put on a hard hat and steel-toed shoes and go out with them. I would embrace the product by having them take me through the process. I was curious and wanted to know the basic concepts to be able explain it intelligently to the customers.

When I joined Mattel a few years later, I found a bigger pond, a place where there were fish out of water from all over the world. It was like I had finally found my watering hole.

At Mattel, I quickly discovered a mentor, another Cuban-American woman who was president of the Latin American division. I took a special interest in getting things done for her and the Latin American division. Three years later, my mentor offered me a job supervising the forecasting and planning division. That was the beginning of my stimulating career.

Think of the ways you've blazed trails simply by putting yourself out there. It's one of the gifts of being different from the rest—you get to show what you're made of, and in the process, you bring that resilience and clarity of vision to the work you do. It's a win-win.

Celebrate your style. Katherine Hepburn hit the scene in the 1930s with a look Hollywood hadn't seen before. Outspoken, intellectual, and witty, Hepburn defied the era's blonde bombshell stereotype. She flouted the fashion rules of the day, preferring tailored pantsuits to more popular revealing dresses, tight girdles, and stockings. "Stockings are an invention of the Devil," she once declared. When RKO staff took away her slacks one day to force her into a skirt, she walked the lot in her underwear until her clothes were returned. Hepburn broke the rules with her style, which became her signature and influenced generations of women. Calvin Klein honored Hepburn in 1986 with a lifetime achievement award from the Council of Fashion Designers. Klein said, "In 1930, she wore pants and suits considered scandalous; today, they are sensational. They've prompted generations of fashion designers to capture her vitality and spirit." Hepburn was a fish out of water by being ahead of her time.

As a fish out of water who wants to be part of it all, it pays to compromise where you can while staying true to yourself.

As the saying goes, you have to choose your battles, and as a fish out of water who wants to be a part of it all, it pays to compromise where you can while staying true to yourself.

Sometimes, dress codes may need to be broken to honestly represent who you are; your ability to do that will depend on your workplace and position. Other times, you can adapt your look for the most harmonious collaboration. Notice what people at your office are wearing and make sure your look says, "I can play the part." You can show your style by the colors you choose and by how you accessorize. Something as small as an interesting watch or a fashion-forward pair of shoes or tie can say, "I'm so much more than what you think I am."

When I moved from Atlanta to L.A., I had to adapt my look to fit in with the business environment of the entertainment industry. I wasn't going to walk into a meeting at E! Entertainment Television wearing pearls and a matched skirt suit when my clients wore jeans. I wore a pants suit and a funky top, and I wore my hair loose instead of coiffed as I'd become used to doing in Atlanta. I compromised a little but never left myself behind.

Today, there are variations, but there's always a running theme: I'm creative, and I like to show it. As a brand strategist and digital marketing executive, I align with what I can relate to in a client's culture and I keep the expression my own. At MTV, I wear jeans and a tailored jacket. At Lifetime, I wear a dress. At Bloomberg, I'm in a suit. But I'm always original in how I accessorize. I wear vintage jewelry and scarves, many of them family heirlooms. Sometimes, I wear chunky turquoise Native American jewelry reflective of my new life in the Southwest. My accessories are conversation pieces, and answering questions about them creates connection and expands comfort zones.

When I travel, I keep an eye out for unusual pieces that interest me. In Guatemala, for instance, I picked up a long silver chain that is used to wrap around wedding couples. I wrap it around my neck and leave a length of chain dangling. It reflects my interest in other cultures and in travel; it's creative, fresh, and original. It's an expression of who I am. For men, it's the tie, the great shirt, the haircut, or the eyeglasses that say *this is who I am*. Be tasteful, and make the look yours.

Be tasteful, and make the look yours.

In Step 1, Jason Heller described how important it was for him to remain steadfast in maintaining who he is at heart. Along with that, how Jason dressed—adapting the dress code to his needs—meant wearing the suit but holding out on the tie.

You can be a scrappy alternative thinker whose bottom line is living with passion and being real.

When I started my own hip-hop record company in my early 20s, I needed to fit in with the musicians I recorded. So I dressed the part. I also learned to talk the part to mix better with my clients. The high road to harmony was to adopt what worked for me—the lingo—and leave the gangster attitude to the others.

When I joined a corporate Internet marketing firm a few years later, it was time to recreate myself again. I sought harmony without giving up what distinguishes me—I'm a scrappy, alternative thinker whose bottom line is living with passion and being real—but the compromises were different. I lost the hip-hop in my speech, speaking slowly and carefully for a time to be sure the slang didn't slip out, and I wore the suit expected of executives there. But I didn't want to look like everyone else because I wasn't like everyone else, and I wanted to be sure that was clear. So, I never wore a tie, although everyone else did.

My last corporate gig was as managing director of Horizon Interactive, a digital marketing firm. The agency is progressive and edgy; it stands out from the competition, and so do I.

Being a hip-hop kid from the Bronx in the corporate world was both liberating and uncomfortable. I feel *equally a fish out of water in the hip-hop world as I do running an Internet marketing firm with corporate guys. But nothing was going to stop me from doing what I set out to do. I feel I have a clarity of vision that's different from other peoples'. Then, I create a tangible path to accomplish that vision. There are two sides to me: creative and business. I don't let society define me. I work solely based on my passions and motivations in life.*

Thom Beers, too, is a fish out of water driven by his passion. When Thom became a TV executive after being a Broadway stage actor for years, the right choice for him was to break with the dress code by wearing a suit when no one else was.

Yet, Thom isn't your average man in a suit, and his credentials prove it. He is founder, CEO, and executive producer of Original Productions, the TV production company known for several hit series, including *Monster Garage*, *Ice Road Truckers*, and the Emmy-nominated *Deadliest Catch*. He has earned a reputation as one of the most creative and successful independent producers in TV today. He's a storyteller and television innovator who emphasizes real people doing extraordinary things. But he's not always been a creative maverick.

Make your statement more important than a dress code.

Years ago, when I left the stage to pursue a career as an executive with Turner Broadcasting, I felt I had a distance to go to be taken seriously. To bridge the gap between actor and executive, I chose to wear a suit and tie while

> others in programming dressed down. My statement was more important to me than adhering to a dress code. I wore a suit and tie every day when I worked at Turner, even if others didn't. I had places to go. So I wore accoutrements that communicated respect. I had ambitions for business. I had a creative side but wanted to be respected for both.
>
> Today, I run my business in jeans and an untucked shirt. I'm dressed for anything—a shoot in Africa or a client meeting. My look says, "I'm ready for adventure."

"You have to make yourself relevant."

Intention is important when it comes to how you present yourself at work. As Thom Beers says, your style should be relevant. Don't wear an eyebrow piercing to the job at the bank. Maybe a favorite necklace or a hip pair of eyeglasses will give you the same good feeling of proclaiming who you are while you integrate into the cultural climate of your workplace. If your office is filled with younger people, don't try to pull off the looks they do. Choose what fits for *you* and is a match for your company or profession. You already stand out. Do it beautifully.

You already stand out. Do it beautifully.

News flash: People can see right through you. If you're a fish out of water who is dressing provocatively to stand out, be warned that people can see right through you, and the message you're sending is "desperate." It's not authentic, and you're not fooling anyone.

Your wardrobe should not be intended to shock or create sensation (unless you're someone like Madonna, and your outrageous outfits help further your career!).

I once knew a man who went to meetings barefoot in the height of the dot-com boom. He was the creator of a successful Internet company, and he seemed to feel he could do whatever he wanted. He was riding high. True, he was a casual sort of guy who liked to go barefoot so in that way it was authentic for him, but going barefoot at work created a sensation. He didn't filter or consider what was appropriate. He crossed the line from authentic to unmannered. His standing out was manufactured, and no one bought it. Instead of gaining their respect, his actions turned people off. Coincidently, the company failed.

How about a little spring cleaning? What do you wear to work? Does it "fit" you? Does it describe you in any way? If it isn't an honest expression, if you feel stifled or false, like you're trying to blend in (when you really don't), or if you're purposely dressing to call more attention to yourself, then it's time to pack up a few bags, give them away, and go shopping.

If you compromise your core, you lose yourself.

Compromise a little, keep a whole lot. The challenge—and the opportunity—when you're a fish out of water comes when you compromise for the sake of harmony but without trying to blend in. How do you do this? You know your core values and you stand by them. That's the distinguishing line. If you compromise your core, you lose yourself.

Core values are the foundation on which a truly successful life is built.

Many of your values change throughout your life, necessarily, as your circumstances change. But your core values, the ones that mean the most to you, remain, manifesting themselves in different ways as you get older. Your core values reflect your deepest, most heartfelt needs. Core values are the foundation on which a truly successful life is built. When you know your core values and live by them, you can trust yourself not to settle for less than you deserve. You can return to those values when it's time to make decisions, and you can trust the decisions you make.

Mark Zuckerberg is another extraordinary example of a Fearless Fish out of water. At 20 years of age, he showed up in Palo Alto, California, with nothing to his name. Four years later, he's running the number one social networking site for young adults and turning down multibillion dollar offers to buy his company, Facebook. Today, the site is used by more than 80 million active users at thousands of high schools, universities, and companies around the world.

Analysts think Zuckerberg could be the nation's richest man under 25, with a net worth estimated at $1.5 billion. His critics think he's a kid who doesn't get that the time to sell is now—a cocky youngster crazy to turn down a $1 billion offer. But Zuckerberg, a geeky fish out of water who's happy sleeping on an unmade mattress and eating cereal with a plastic spoon, wants to hunker down and do it his way. "I'm here to build something for the long term," he says. "Anything else is a distraction."

Zuckerberg and his top executives have the faith that open, collaborative information sharing can make the world a better place. They're not bowing to the corporate giants who think they know better. "As a company," Zuckerberg told *Time* magazine in July 2007, "we're very focused on what we're building and not as focused on the exit. We just believe that we're adding a certain amount of value to people's lives if we build a very good product. That's the reason why more than half of our users use the product every day—it's a more efficient way for them to communicate with their friends and get information about the people around them than anything else they can do. We're not really looking to sell the company. We're not looking to IPO anytime soon. It's just not the core focus of the company." Recently, Zuckerberg sold a minuscule 1.6 percent piece of Facebook to Microsoft for $240 million—giving him the financial freedom to support his unique vision and values.

What are your core values? Can you list them in a snap? When you know your core values that well you can be sure you're living by them, or you can make adjustments if you discover you've compromised too much for your own good. My main core values are love, safety, and living with integrity. They guide me to spend as much time as I can with my daughter, to see my sister and father as often as I can, to be sure my family's finances are secure, and to live an honest, well-intentioned life. Try listing your core values and then look for overlap and narrow the list to the primary three or four. Remember these. Live by them. They are your life support when you're a fish out of water.

Let others shine the light on you. Remember Wilbur, E.B. White's famous pig? The message there goes way beyond a children's story. Wilbur would have been nothing without Charlotte's praise for him in her web. Her actions were miraculous and attracted attention. They said, "You may not believe in him, but I do." And everyone took notice, even Wilbur. ("Really? *I'm* terrific?")

It helps to have someone around who "gets" you.

It helps to have someone around who "gets" you, especially when it's someone you admire. These people can help strengthen your trust in yourself and show others you're someone to notice.

I've always had an advocate cheering me on, someone who supported me and who I could also learn from.

During one of my first jobs at the alternative newspaper *Creative Loafing,* my supporter was a dynamic salesman, a real closer. With a bigger-than-life presence, Scott Walsey commanded the room, telling the clients why they had to be in the pages of the newspaper with so much enthusiasm they just had to buy. I absorbed it all and wove his style into mine, increasing my confidence as I did. Beyond teaching me the ropes, he told my skeptical coworkers that I was the real deal. His advocacy sealed my success at the paper.

If no one advocates for you now, look for the person in your office or your field that you can establish a connection with, someone who gets you and could be interested in seeing you do well. Communicate your interest and admiration, and open yourself to that individual. Both of you can gain from it. Especially the mentor who gets that special satisfaction that comes from passing on wisdom.

Having others shine a light on you has other benefits, as well; it can alleviate the loneliness you may feel as a fish out of water. There's nothing like having people around who you feel connection with, and you can take that feeling with you everywhere you go. For the past 15 years, I've hosted a dinner for bright, ambitious women from around the country who advocate for each other. They come to reconnect. We appreciate each other's experience and abilities, and we help reinforce our value to each other and to others in our field when we see an opportunity.

I met this group of marketing executives in the early days of starting my own company, when I traveled to cable television conventions and marketing conferences to go after business. I walked the convention floor, shopping my portfolio, getting to know the players, trying to sell people on what I could do for them. I was a pioneer as an independent and a woman; everyone else had a network or cable company behind them. To deepen the connections and create community at these out-of-town events, I invited several of the women I met for a "girls' night out"—a networking dinner I'd host at a great restaurant. These 8 or 10 heads of marketing from different networks swapped stories and realized that they had quite a lot in common. We got to know each other's talents and experiences and became great advocates for each other in every way.

When you shine a light on who you are, those who see you fully will want to come into *your* circle. Or they'll want to give you a hand or a piece of good advice. Remember Nathalie Lubensky from Step 1? She's SVP of affiliate marketing at Disney and ESPN Media Networks. She had that experience. After moving up through the ranks, she found herself the only woman of color and the only mother in her division, and she needed an ally.

I pride myself on delivering "the real deal." I'm intuitive, I trust my gut, and I'm known for telling the truth when it's needed. I rose to the top of Disney and ESPN Media Networks by being frank, and that wasn't always popular. But I am used to being a fish out of water. I don't assume I'll fit in when I walk into a room, and I don't apologize for who I am when I get there.

When I took this job, I was confronted with a new challenge: Everyone was into sports and I wasn't.

Before giving a big PowerPoint presentation to ESPN execs, I needed an advocate. I tried connecting with my boss about the Super Bowl but found it just wasn't me. I couldn't do it. So, I decided to approach him my way, to connect with him person to person. One day, I initiated a frank discussion with my boss. I told him a little about my background and what it was like juggling motherhood and this job. I was authentic, not apologetic and not asking for pity. My show of vulnerability created a connection.

What helped me was spending time with my new boss. I told him about the real me, the trials and tribulations. I knew I needed him to be my advocate more than anyone else. The outcome is that my boss became my advocate going into the presentation and long after it.

I didn't have to be a jock or talk about the Super Bowl to get what I needed. All I had to do was be authentic, to shine a light on who I am: honest, gutsy, resilient, determined, someone who can lead a group of people who are nothing like me. I'm upfront and outspoken, I get attention, and it works for me and for the company.

After my son Luc was born, I was sent to San Diego for a senior staff meeting. I set the stage for what was to be the best year of my personal and professional life. I showed a lot of courage and spoke honestly. I was in a room full of men, but I can have the biggest balls because I call out the problems. I deliver the real deal, telling the truth in an organization where people generally try not to stir things up.

As the only Jamaican-American in the executive ranks of Tribune, Vinnie Malcolm also discovered the value of having an advocate put the spotlight on him.

My high school certificate says, "Marches to his own beat." And that was okay with me; I didn't need everyone to follow along. I was a fish out of water for most of my youth in Jamaica, and when I finally landed in New York, I found it tough to make friends because the kids didn't know where I fit in.

Most blacks who are successful are Ivy Leaguers or former jocks. I had to figure out how I was going to get ahead without these advantages. I attribute my success to having an advocate, someone who smoothed out the rough areas. My former boss grew up on the south side of Chicago, so he was comfortable with me from the start. He identified with my potential and, because he was color-blind, he guided me up through the ranks, grooming me for a station manager position. My boss was a great mentor to me. If you're different, you need a mentor—at least in the beginning—to smooth the rough areas.

Be an inspiration. Differences are an essential part of life—there isn't a leaf or a rock or a bird or a person exactly like another. Each of us has something beautifully unique to offer the world; and variety makes it work. If they hadn't stayed true to their values, Katherine Hepburn would have been just another good actress, and Ellen DeGeneres would have gone back to doing stand-up in small clubs. Thom Beers would have remained a struggling actor in New York and never gone on to make some of America's most popular television shows. None of the fish out of water who've lived fearlessly and made a difference would have fulfilled their soul's purpose if they had given in to cultural pressure to conform or surrendered before even starting.

You don't want to squeeze yourself into being someone you're not.

I have huge admiration for fish out of water. We're the survivors. We don't want to squeeze ourselves into being people we're not. We don't look for the cracks to fit into, and we know we couldn't fit into the cracks if we tried. We've shown courage in getting this far and in choosing positions we want, even if we don't blend in. We've accepted that we march to our own beat.

When you stand out from the pack, people take a second look at you. You're intriguing. You bring a freshness with you, the possibility for change. You inspire curiosity. You attract attention. You're unforgettable. Live it big. Shine a light on who you are and what you do in your own brave, beautiful, unique way and you'll attract attention in a way that really matters. Chances are you'll inspire others, too, with how you live your differences.

Step 2 Exercises

You can't be unforgettable unless you dare to be different.

What's different about you that stands out and can be positively illuminated?

_____

_____

_____

_____

It's helpful to remind yourself of what you are known for, your area of expertise, so that you can shine a light on the strengths of these attributes. Write down what you are an expert in, what you can do better than others around you.

_____

_____

_____

_____

What personal interest can you build on that could expand your sphere of influence inside your organization or industry?

_____

_____

_____

_____

What does your personal style say about you? Does it communicate who you are inside and shine a light on your differences?

Men
   Ties

   _____

   Suits

   _____

   Shirts

   _____

   Pants

   _____

   Bag/Brief Case

   _____

   Shoes

   _____

Women
   Suits

   _____

Shirts

_____

Pants

_____

Skirts

_____

Bag/Brief Case

_____

Shoes

_____

What perceptions are out there about you that you could change for the better? Name three:

1. _____
2. _____
3. _____

How will you change those perceptions about you?

_____
_____
_____
_____

Who in your work life can shine a light on you?

_____
_____

How can you be an inspiration to others in your organization or industry?

_____

_____

_____

_____

Step 3

Find a Few Fish Like You

Fearless Fish Out of Water Get in the Swim by Discovering Connections

- Discover your comfort zones.
- Align with someone on the inside.
- Lead the charge.
- Show you're a fan.

Many years ago, I made a decision to stop beating myself up for not being perfect. This moment of clarity was triggered by the end of yet another failed personal relationship. To accomplish this seemingly impossible goal, my friend Kim Youngblood suggested I go to the Esalen Institute in Big Sur (this is where the human potential movement started in the 1960s), take a workshop, and get on the path to self-awareness.

After combing through a huge booklet packed with workshops focusing on everything from yoga, vision painting, and dream analysis to relationships and communication, I zeroed in on "Letting Go and Moving On."

During the weeklong gestalt workshop, we were asked to choose our biggest demon, and then talk to it as if it were a person. My demon was "Judgment." There I was, sitting with Judgment (a pillow propped up on a chair), telling it I was hurt by its harsh assessment of my actions. After all, I was just a human with flaws like everyone else. I was tired of Judgment holding me to a higher standard and making me feel inadequate—and, at times, worthless. I tried to convince Judgment I was just different from everyone, that I needed to be understood, to be appreciated. And that's when the light bulb went on. It had to start with me. If I accepted myself, others would, too.

In the days that followed, I formed friendships with a few people in the group who encouraged me to open up and share moments in my life that were—until this point— secrets. When they told me their stories, I made myself listen without prejudice and found I liked my new friends, warts and all. Would I be accepted if I came clean? On the last day of the workshop, I took a chance and spilled everything about my mother, my lost childhood, and my failure to love anyone fully. And you know what? I received acceptance. Now I had a chance to do the same for myself. It all came from seeking support from people who were like me—not perfect, and wanting to feel okay about it.

When I told one of my girlfriends this story, she flatly said, "I'd rather stick needles in my eye than do a workshop at Esalen." I had to laugh at the truth in that statement. Owning who you are to a group of strangers isn't easy, but that's exactly what we do when we commit to spending a minimum of 40 hours each week working side-by-side with people in business. They see you every day and judge you based on how you react to difficult situations. How well you perform in front of them can be improved by aligning yourself with people who can guide you and by putting yourself in situations that are familiar.

Step 3 on the path to fearlessness is to discover where, when, and what you find comfort in so you can anchor yourself in your own uniqueness. It's also about finding other people like you— yes, they do exist—and leading the way for them to become accepted. After all, it's exhausting to always be outside your comfort zone day in and day out. Finding people who align with your sensibilities can make all the difference.

In the previous two steps, we discussed going fishing for the real you and using your differences as a lure. As we discovered, authenticity will always be the keystone for unlocking the real you. That's what your coworkers will gravitate to. Attempt anything else and they'll see through your act and start treating you accordingly.

Remember my friend David, the limo driver I mentioned in Step 2? When he walked into the company offices for the first time, he stepped into a very different world. David is very neat, organized, and self-contained. The environment he walked into was loud, crass, disorganized, and the people were rather unkempt—whether they were male or female. David was not about to retrofit himself to fit into this environment, yet he knew that he could also be seen as putting on airs, appearing superior to his fellow drivers. So, he used his sense of humor as an icebreaker, and he asked for help whenever he needed it from whoever was nearby. In this way, the rest of the crew got to know him, and they never felt that he thought he was above anyone. David also admitted his mistakes openly and took everyone's ribbing in a jocular way. When he left the company, a lot of people came to say good-bye—and he'd never changed his principles. Instead, he found ways to fit in, remain true to himself, and rise to the occasion.

Once you're on track with a better understanding of yourself—accepting yourself for your differences, showing your strengths, celebrating your style with grace and confidence, and learning to let others shine a light on you—you'll become the inspiration you were meant to be. And I don't mean in a self-aggrandizing manner, but someone who is completely comfortable in her skin, doesn't apologize for who she is, and thinks nothing of living life her own way!

A great example of someone who has always maintained his core identity is Zeev Haskal, owner of Mega Group, one of the top 10—out of 20,000—investigative firms in California. He was completely out of his element when he moved from Israel to Los Angeles, but he found a small community to help him fit in.

I was born and raised in Ramat-Gan, Israel. I was a bit of a wild kid, unlike my brother who did what our parents told him—I rebelled against them all the time. So, I was sent to a professional school to study electronics and computers. I hated every minute of it. What I liked was sports and music.

When I came to L.A., I didn't have many friends. I didn't know anyone who could help me at work. My English was so bad I wasn't allowed to answer the phone.

L.A. has a small Israeli community and the same kind of weather as Israel, so it wasn't totally unfamiliar. A few of the Israelis I met helped me in various ways and gave me a foundation. I set out to learn the English language and integrate myself into the American culture. I wanted to be corrected by my girlfriends when I said something that was wrong. Just because I speak with an accent doesn't mean I think with my accent. I'd look at people driving fancy cars and ask myself, "How did they get it and how can I get there?" instead of being jealous.

My creativity has contributed to my success. That's what's helped me reinvent myself. It's about results. I started as a rebellious kid, and now I'm a successful businessman.

Going into anything with expectations is going to hamstring your efforts and leave you feeling disappointed.

Zeev's journey to success wasn't easy. To smooth the way he aligned with other Israelis and then broke out to embrace the larger business community. All he had to do was take the first step and reach out.

When you're venturing into unknown territory, try to stay as neutral as possible. Going into anything with expectations is going to hamstring your efforts and leave you feeling disappointed Stay open to the possibilities and amp up your faith to keep yourself from saying, "This stuff doesn't work," "I'm not cut out for this," "This will take forever," "I don't have the stamina or patience," or "I'll never get through to these people."

News flash: Complaints are just that—complaints. When thoughts like these begin filling your head, it's time to write a new script for yourself. As a Fearless Fish out of water, you don't have the time or energy to waste on complaining—you've got too much opportunity in front of you to focus on! Granted, there will be those days when you feel like the world is trying to squash you like a bug. That's the time to remember who you are: an exceptionally creative person and *a fish out of water*. This adversity is par for the course, and you've got the wherewithal to not only get through it but to go beyond it.

Owner of Original Productions, Thom Beers, mentioned in Step 2, had a lot of challenges when growing up, but he had a much different attitude working for him.

I have been a fish out of water my whole life. My family lived in upstate New York in a little crackerbox house. When I was seven or eight, my mother was sitting with some women friends talking about where they'd be in five years. She said, "If I'm still living here in five years—I'll kill myself!"

The majority of people where I grew up never leave home. Few people have a sense of wanderlust. Some kids look at National Geographic *and see the pretty animals in Africa—I wasn't content to just look. I wanted to go there.*

When I moved to Atlanta, I felt like a fish out of water. For me, that feeling never stops. I love that saying, "Wherever you go, there you are." That speaks to feeling good about yourself.

Fish out of water don't have a herd mentality.

Swimming against the stream—now, there's a thought! Sometimes, it seems much of the world is like one giant herd of cattle heading in the same direction—everyone thinking the same way, living life according to the accepted methods. Fish out of water don't have that herd mentality. They're about soaring when everyone else is plodding along. But while you're up there flying, it would be nice if you had some company, and that's where this step comes in: finding a few fish just like you.

Discover your comfort zone. When you become involved in what interests you or get active in areas where you already feel comfortable, you're in familiar territory—your comfort zone.

One thing I want to stress is that using comfort zones is not about hiding out from people, challenges, and situations. They're also not to be used as a survival mechanism. Instead, comfort zones are about knowing your likes and dislikes so you can function as optimally as possible in any situation. In the case of working for an organization, it's about using your comfort zone as a springboard for getting involved and engaged with your organization.

If you're a fish out of water, easing your way in gives you confidence, and at the same time, strengthens business relationships.

If you're a fish out of water, easing your way in gives you confidence, and at the same time, strengthens business relationships. While at Turner Broadcasting, I once volunteered to be in an off-site company talent show with others who, like me, loved being onstage. I sang a funny old song and then performed with my coworkers in *a Saturday Night Live*-type skit. No one knew I had these talents before my appearance. Taking the stage took courage and it put the spotlight on my fearless nature. The bonding experience with everyone who put on the show and those in the audience changed perceptions of me and enhanced my career.

Harold "H" Lewis is another Fearless Fish who found his comfort zone with some colleagues. He's an African-American and top executive at The Weather Channel Interactive, and he got comfortable in his new role by connecting with other employees of color. "We'd have lunch out of the building and share our experiences. I'd ask how others in the organization viewed my work group. Their insights were invaluable," he said.

To discover your comfort zone, start by making a list of who and what makes you feel comfortable. Second, determine *why* those people and things make you feel comfortable. How do they make you feel? Respected, appreciated, confident, an integral part of the team, energized, creative, intelligent, wise, insightful, skilled, valuable, constructive, practical, ahead of the pack, iconoclastic? You can derive loads of positive feelings when you stop to consider why any particular comfort zone is in place. Be aware, though, if what's behind a comfort zone is fear or pain, then you need to let go of that particular comfort zone. It will only hold you back from being more authentic and reaching your potential.

News flash: Introspection doesn't require therapeutic intervention. This is just about getting real with yourself. The key phrase is "be authentic." Your greatest gift to yourself and the world—in any arena—is to be who you truly are, with honesty and integrity. When you are being yourself, you literally shine.

An important aspect of the introspection process involves learning to see yourself with honesty.

An important aspect of the introspection process involves learning to see yourself with honesty. By doing that, self-acceptance becomes easier and easier as you discover, along with a clear understanding of your comfort zones, what is working for you and what isn't.

Next, identify which of your comfort zones is part of your everyday work life and which you might need to create or expand upon. Maybe you're into sports and your company has a baseball team you could join. Another possibility is to volunteer for an internal council or a committee that is working on a plum project that interests you. If you're an entrepreneur, get active in industry organizations. If you haven't done it already, do what you need to clear your calendar so you have the time to join the group, project, or endeavor that resonates with the *real* you.

My suggestion to find your comfort zone is designed to anchor you so you don't flounder in rough seas.

For fish out of water, being uncomfortable or feeling disconnected can be a way of life. Finding your comfort zone is a surefire way to give yourself an anchor so you don't flounder in rough seas. If you're going through a period where everything is new and different and you just can't find anything that feels right, stay with those feelings—don't stuff them down to where they disappear and can't be felt or recognized for what they are anymore. Your emotions are clues. You have them for a reason.

Ignoring or denying them is like barreling past a sign that says, "Bridge is out"— you're headed for possible disaster.

If you pay attention to your feelings, you'll have a much better chance at clearly seeing what's in front of you and also seeing the opportunities at hand. You may discover something you didn't know before. Revel in the chance to learn something new about yourself. The universe may have meant this moment in your life to be what shakes you up and forces you to go deeper; to shed your tough, stubborn, or shy exterior and really feel what it's like to be alive and engaged.

Revel in the chance to learn something new about yourself.

Susan O'Meara, an American documentary filmmaker currently living in Ireland, started out life in a world where individuality and thinking outside the box were stifled. She eventually had to come to terms with what she felt deep inside herself and then take a stand.

I have always felt like a fish out of water. Except now, I like it.

I went to Catholic grade school in central California, grades one through six—straitlaced, four-eyed (black glasses), strictly ponytailed and a bookworm, I believed the nuns. And there's no one like a nun to make you feel like you (1) don't belong, but (2) you better fit in . . . or else.

It's taken me a long time to get where I'm going and find out what I'm about. Being an individual isn't about rules, regulations, or repression. It's about filling yourself with the freedom to embrace frailties and fabulousness and forgiveness simultaneously. And spreading that humanity. We are all special. We are all one of a kind. That's really something.

Being fully yourself means discovering, making, or writing your own blueprint. Then you can live simultaneously as both a fish out of water and a fish in the water. And swim wherever you like.

Everything that happens in your life is truly in your best interest.

News flash: It's time to believe that the next step will be a better one. No matter what your situation, you have options available. It's a matter of going for it. Maybe you've been laid off, or you've decided to leave your company and you're once again out there on your own. Become fearless by setting your intention each day and finding something that brings you back to what's positively different about you. Then, seek people or places of comfort as you navigate your next move. Everyone I know who has successfully made it through a jobless period has seen it as an opportunity to be with their kids more, have weekly lunches with old colleagues and vendors, show up at industry events where they know people ("See, I'm not dead!"), travel to amazing destinations, volunteer for causes important to them, and realized it was time to move on after all.

As we learned in Step 1, fish out of water are truly unique and because of their uniqueness, they will not always be able to fit in. Not every company or organization is able to work with us because their business focus, arena, and/or leaders may not allow it. Our only choice then is to take our uniqueness somewhere else and showcase our talents where they will be recognized for what they are: needed and worthy of being celebrated. It all comes down to clearly understanding who we are and what we have to offer—and the right job *will* appear!

Everything that happens in your life is truly in sync with your destiny. It may feel painful at first, but it could be that you need change in your life and you just don't know it. Perhaps it's time to re-evaluate your career choice and path and determine what it is you really want to be doing. Maybe you need to reorganize your thinking and sense of purpose in life. What would the impact be on you and those around you? What kind of person could you become if you supported the genuine you?

For several decades now, major car companies have laid off tens of thousands of employees. In some families, working for the same company has been generational: grandfathers, fathers, and sons working side by side—no other skills were developed except those required at the plant. When the layoffs hit, it created major upheaval for the affected individuals and their families.

Many former employees floundered, unable to shift into a new life. They were one-trick ponies. Their sense of self-esteem completely deflated, they withdrew into alcohol, drugs, and depression. Families suffered terribly and never recovered.

Other laid-off workers took a look around and decided to make the best of the situation. Some opted to get involved with computers, real estate, the stock market, or new businesses. Others decided to go for the brass ring and followed their hearts. They redirected their lives by seeing the opportunity before them. Yes, time was required to go through the transition period, and sometimes that was rough going; but they persevered and came out on top. They reinvented themselves.

That's exactly what happened when 12 former cannery workers—mostly in their mid-40s—were laid off in December 2006 from the Birds Eye Foods plant near Santa Cruz, California. They attended the Shoreline School of Cosmetology and graduated alongside young adults. Although they toiled away for years in the cannery out of loyalty and necessity, most of their dreams involved working for an upscale salon and building a clientele close to home. These dreams would never have been realized had it not been for their company's downsizing.[1]

The period between jobs is a gift to help you unwrap your real dreams and desires and to reveal what's next in your life. Seeing it any other way is negative thinking. This is your chance to decide whether you even like the career path you've chosen. Does it make you feel comfortable and challenged all at once? It should. Because this is it. This is your life and the majority of every hour of every day is spent working, so why spend it in a business or on a career that creates fear, unhappiness, and a sense of inadequacy or failure?

As a business owner, I know that my comfort zone is engaged when I'm working with like-minded clients. If you know what kind of people you like to work with, you can go after them more specifically by writing down the qualities they possess. There is power in the pen, and writing down your intention on paper can bring those people to you. Writing things down is like a declaration: This is what I stand for, this is who I like to work with, this is where I'm going. It's a constant reminder of where your focus is, and your daily attitude is going to reflect that.

Here's an example of where my company and I got off track because of external influences that challenged who we are and what we're about. We *let* ourselves get pushed out of our comfort zone and paid the price.

In 2006, business had gotten slow and some of our employees had started to panic, which in turn made me worry. I had learned after years and years in the

---

[1] www.santacruzsentinel.com/ci_9836670

ad game that this industry has a definite roller coaster ride component to it, but this time, everything seemed to have come to a screeching halt. Desperation set in and we started pitching new business like mad.

A major television network we had never worked with arrived on the scene wanting to build a web site for a new reality show. The client was big, blustery, and rude—not our ideal client profile. He wanted to let us know how experienced he was and bragged about his accomplishments. Even though we saw right through his facade, we took the business.

One Friday afternoon he said, "If you can't show me a layout I like on Monday, you're fired." So, instead of telling him we'd be pleased if he'd fire us, we begged for another chance and worked all weekend to save the account. He loved what we produced and the madness continued. The project consumed our company and negatively impacted morale as he was rude on almost every call and kept changing direction.

When we delivered the completed web site to him, he announced that he would not pay a quarter of our bill because the process had been so difficult for him. For him!

From that day forward, we decided to define our ideal client profile and the types of projects we wanted to attract. Miraculously, business started pouring in, and 2007 was our best year ever.

It's important for you to stay positive as you're finding your comfort zone; otherwise your efforts can have the opposite effect.

I've noticed that when I'm feeling good about myself and my work, I attract the right kind of clients. When I'm beating myself up and feeling impoverished, clients arrive on the scene that treat me poorly. It's important for you to stay positive as you're finding your comfort zone, otherwise your efforts can have the opposite effect.

If you can't find your comfort zone inside your company or outside in your industry, create it.

If you can't find your comfort zone inside your company or your industry, create it. If you are environmentally conscious, start a green initiative with others who have the same passion. If you're politically active, find people who share your point of view and involve them in your cause. That's what Evan Shapiro, executive vice president and general manager of Independent Film Channel (IFC) does. He's put his cable channel on the map by underscoring its position as "Voices of Independent Culture." During the 2008 election, Evan created his own political blog where he invited commentary from people inside and outside of his channel, making sure to air programming on IFC that focused on independent political thinking. The effort solidified a loyal viewing audience and generated a lot of positive press for Shapiro and his team. Connection comes from involvement, and involvement leads to inclusion.

When you show your expertise, your comfort and self-assurance grow, and the splash can be heard from all the way outside the circle.

We're in our comfort zone when we're confident, and we're typically confident when we're doing something we know we're good at. In most jobs, there are things we know so well we could do them with our eyes closed, and other things that are just outside our areas of mastery. Try to do one thing every day in your area of mastery, and if that's not possible—if you're in a new job or new in a field—add in something that gives you a feeling of ease and confidence because you're already great at it. It could be that you're an ace at making peace when coworkers disagree, or you can see instantly how to organize a project, or you have a knack for rallying the troops to focus on a goal and get it done. When you show your expertise, your comfort and self-assurance grow, and the splash can be heard from all the way outside the circle.

Over time, comfort zones will shift. Why? Because we are constantly growing and changing—it's part of our nature. New comfort zones may develop; old ones will no longer be needed. As you experience the benefits and possible drawbacks of some comfort zones, they may become more or less necessary. Always keep in mind that as you change, so will your needs. Until then, look for someone on the inside of your company or industry who can take you by the hand and mentor you, or become a mentor yourself.

Having connection with someone on the inside can help you broaden your realm of acceptance.

Align with someone on the inside. Denzel Washington—a Fearless Fish out of water—knows what it means to have a mentor, someone who is interested in you. He believes that "We get where we're going with a push from someone who cares." Mentors, allies, cheerleaders of any kind—all of them play an important role when you're a fish out of water. Having connection with someone on the inside can help you broaden your realm of acceptance.

It's time to cultivate these kinds of valuable relationships. To start, invite someone you admire to grab a cup of coffee one morning. (If you don't ask, the answer will always be no!) When you're out together, tell that person you'd like to be more a part of things at work and ask for advice. You don't have to follow every suggestion, but listen closely and be appreciative of whatever suggestions are offered.

When Kim Deck, whom you learned about in Step 1, was launching her career, she asked for help from some of the experts. They were happy to have her shadow them, and by doing so, she learned from the best. The bonus was that they got to know her, too, and saw what she could do, leading to her easier integration at the firm.

Erica Huggins credits her rise to senior executive VP of Imagine Entertainment (Ron Howard and Brian Grazer's company) to her mentors, Janice Hampton and Robert Cort.

> *I got a job working on the movie* Hairspray. *I went to Baltimore and there was Janice, who took me under her wing and taught me how to be a film editor and how to talk to directors and producers. When I started, I was her first assistant—but she treated me as an equal. I made myself invaluable to her. When she would stop to cut the film, I would chop it and tape it for her. I would make elaborate charts for her so she could see her progress. I created a world for her to work within, one in which she could have more fun. At the time, I didn't know I was in a mentoring relationship. I just wanted someone to pay attention to me.*

My second mentor, Robert Cort, was a producer on my last movie with Janice. He asked me if I wanted to be a producer. He loved editing movies, which was unusual, so he appreciated my talents. He was making a deal with Polygram, the first international studio coming to Hollywood. Robert was CEO of Innerscope, and he had to build out that company as an anchor for Polygram.

I made a deal with Robert: If he was going to make a change, he had to figure out how to do it—and I was the right person to help him do just that. So, for three months I was like a sponge, learning all I could from him. I went to his lunches, sat in on his meetings, listened to his phone calls. And he paid me exactly the same as I was getting as an editor. Our deal was that after three months, I would become a producer and get a raise. And that's exactly what happened.

He kept his promise. I was with him five years at Innerscope, until it became Radar Pictures, and then I spent another five years helping build Radar. I had been an on-set producer on back-to-back movies until I left and went to Imagine. While all this was going on, I was also a wife and mother of two children.

Now, I'm the mentor as senior executive VP of Imagine. This job is made for me. I've been here three years. I'm the decision maker on making movies—the guide from development to final cut. I wouldn't have gotten that job without relationships.

It's important to choose your mentors carefully and cultivate those relationships over time.

It's important to choose your mentors carefully and cultivate those relationships over time. Let the relationship unfold slowly with someone who believes in you and will cheer you on. Show that person that mentoring is a two-way street by actually taking the advice offered and checking back to let your mentor know the outcome. When things go well, show your appreciation in a handwritten note and, if it feels right, a small gift. Back when I had mentors I didn't have to pay for, I would send all kinds of wonderful, memorable gifts like an antique bowling pin for a mentor who had "bowled me over with good advice," a Chinese take-out container filled with fortune cookies with a note that read, "What good fortune it was for me to meet you," and a stainless steel ice cream bucket and scoop for "Helping to make my life sweeter." Of course, sincerity is key here; otherwise, people will feel you're brownnosing them and resent being manipulated. If you're being authentic, your relationships will deepen, and you will prosper naturally at work, experiencing fulfillment and feeling energized and engaged.

Compassionate leadership benefits everyone and it's the one-on-one coaching of an apprentice that can give more experienced workers increased relevance.

Lead the charge. As valuable as it is to have a mentor, it's even more strategic to become one yourself. What's so nonsensical to me is that some people believe that being a mentor is a one-way street, a time waster. As much lip service as it gets, in reality many executives rarely consider mentoring as an avenue to business success. That's just dead wrong. Compassionate leadership benefits everyone, and it's the one-on-one coaching of an apprentice that can give more experienced workers increased relevance as times change. Learning from younger or less experienced people spurs evolution and creates staying power for the senior members of the team. For the fish out of water, an added benefit is that by generously sharing your own expertise, you become involved and integral.

Mentoring is equally beneficial for women and men, but I often hear women complain that they don't have time to mentor because they have the added burden of juggling work and family. It's grandiose and inauthentic for working women to think that they can be positive role models by simply showing that they're proficient at this balancing act. They have to take time to share experiences and guide young people to their greatest good. It's the right thing to do, especially for the fish out of water that are under the microscope. Fear of someone taking their job or appearing to be too nurturing in front of male coworkers is unfounded. If you're a woman who is not taking time to mentor, I guarantee you that your team, especially its female members, will talk behind your back about your lack of compassion—and that's deadly gossip to a woman trying to secure her stature in an organization.

I've seen this scenario time and time again—especially at women-run companies where mentor programs are created only for customers—and the inside company culture is "mean girls gone corporate." For the Fearless Fish out of water who is also a woman, there must be time put aside for the ones who need you to lend a hand, a shoulder, a kind word of encouragement, or your insight.

For men, the paradigm in place for many generations has been work first at any cost, including the potential alienation of family. Since the onset of the feminist movement, many men have decided that finding balance between work and business is far more important. Men have opted to be more integral to the family dynamic, often taking on household duties typically relegated to women. What this has done for business is bring more emotional sophistication and nuance into the workplace—enhancing a man's ability to effectively mentor.

Today's mentors lead with a wide spectrum of expression and styles. Rather than just the stereotypical wizened crone, sage, or steamrolling tyrant, effective mentors are generous in spirit and advice. You can demonstrate your role as a mentor by hiring more people who are like you. As the first woman of color to head up her department at Disney and ESPN Media Networks, Nathalie Lubensky has hired a multicultural staff, making it a point to mentor others and see to their promotions. Vinnie Malcolm, Tribune Broadcasting's first black general manager, brought in African-American heads of ad sales and marketing. His thinking is: "If you're different, you need a mentor to smooth the rough areas." Annie Trouvé, a French nurse at a U.S. hospital, has mentored so many younger nurses over the years she's really not a fish out of water anymore.

The flip side of this is recognizing the people around you who could be your mentors. Greg Clark, at MTV Networks, says that he's always been disciplined because his father was in the military and taught him well. Greg also looks up to his mother, a great supporter of his dreams who really pushed him.

> *"I look up to both my parents. They're both artists. Because of them, when I began working for MTV Networks and got the hang of things, I could reinvent myself. I'm definitely seen as willing to take risks—and part of risk taking is changing oneself. Because I'm the youngest member of a nearly all-female staff, I was brought in to give my ideas as a young male. A few of our networks cater to young men and being one of the few men in the department, management is looking to me to be a risk taker and make changes. I'm rising to the occasion with the help of those above me who are showing the way."*

The teacher learns by teaching. The fish out of water integrates by helping others who are outside the circle.

Show you're a fan. There are many roads in. I have found that one sure road in is to befriend the head of the company or department and become a champion for his or her vision. It's not about trying to become teacher's pet. It's about being integral to the company, and feeling respected for who you are and what you bring to the table. It's about being different and offering something different, too, something invaluable.

Genuine interest radiates outward and engages other people.

Being a mentor, a leader who is generous in spirit and advice, can be demonstrated by hiring more people who are like you.

As you go about showing you're a fan, one thing to be very clear on is that this is not about establishing allies, which is simply political and superficial. Being a fan is based on your sincere desire to resonate with people and projects, not a way of losing yourself in order to get ahead. Genuine interest radiates outward and engages other people. When you find the right note with people, as H Lewis, whom I mentioned earlier, did, it's amazing how the dynamic of your work relationships expands.

> *I left a 20-person, tech-focused, all-male small business to work for the Weather Channel in Atlanta, which has over 700 employees. I joined a new group in strategy and*

> *development along with other colleagues who were new to the company and new to the industry.*
>
> *Women headed the group. I was used to being around a bunch of guys where you focused on work and connected around sports. At The Weather Channel, though, the first five minutes of every meeting was spent just chatting, typically about non-work-related subjects. I learned to connect around personal interests like dogs. So different. You had to show you cared about people as individuals first, and then we got down to business.*
>
> *With women, there's a lot more talking. Guys talk in shorthand. I had to go from grunting to actually expressing myself. I had to step back and acquaint myself with a new company and new role. I realized that I needed to get out and circulate. You've got to do it in a way that doesn't look like you're just tooting your own horn. It really takes time to build credibility and positive information about you.*

To make a real connection, you first have to tune in to what interests the head of your company or department. The next step is to get involved in it in a useful way. Take a 180-degree turn and stand in your boss's shoes. What are his or her pet projects? What does he or she really want? If you don't know, ask. This kind of focused interest and enthusiasm works to create an unbreakable bond between you and the person who can most influence where you go in the company. Again, this is not about compromising yourself just to ensure you fit in. As I covered in Step 2, *know your core values and stand by them.* That's the distinguishing line. If you compromise your core, you lose yourself. Your actions and choices must truly resonate with who you are.

When I was at Turner Broadcasting, I would have lunch with the heads of each network on a monthly basis. I was just a director and they were presidents, but they were vitally interested in my creative ideas for driving distribution for their networks and how I was leveraging the local power of our affiliates to get people to watch their shows. The lunches were productive, fun, and lively, something to look forward to. I gained insight on what was important to them and supported their goals in a big way with my marketing programs. Essentially, it was about determining what was really working and then building on that.

For example, I pushed through a campaign for CNN Special Reports in which we used FedEx to send timely, topical "hot spots" to affiliates to run locally. This reflected CNN's focus on placing breaking news first and providing comprehensive coverage afterward. To arrive at this strategy, I asked CNN's president, "What do you think your audience isn't 'getting' about your network that they should know?" Today, when I'm dealing with clients, I zero in on what is specifically and uniquely important to them. For instance, if I was working with someone in the pharmaceutical business, I'd ask, "What aren't doctors understanding about the products you're selling?" Questions like this are what your client or managers or bosses want to hear. It means you're taking a keen interest in their agenda, product, and future.

If you're inside a corporation, you may be shaking your head thinking, "There's no way I can get to that level; it's impossible to penetrate the boundaries of the organizational chart or leapfrog over my boss' head." If that's the case, read the company web site, listen carefully to team pep talks from higher ups, and, if you can manage it, introduce yourself at company events and ask at the appropriate juncture in your conversation, "What's keeping you up at night?" The answer should reveal the challenge they need to meet or the special project they want to put into motion. You could be the person to support their efforts.

As an ad agency owner, I often have to work day-to-day with middle management rather than the top brass. To get direction from the top, I schedule meetings around lunch, drinks, or dinner with their bosses, and on a social, friendly basis ask how things are going and what their goals are. I can then translate that intelligence into smart strategies that make my clients look like stars.

Your contributions are valuable and time spent with you is something to look forward to.

When you approach clients and work with them at this level, you have to face any fears you have around making bold moves. Being a Fearless Fish out of water means believing that you are not just taking up space but that your contributions are valuable. Time spent with you is something to look forward to. Cultivating this kind of confidence from deep inside of you (where fearlessness comes from) will spur you forward more than anything else in life. To create that confidence, tell yourself that you are good enough and completely capable, write down what you'll say, practice with a coach or a mentor, and visualize a positive outcome.

When you become more comfortable with how your organization works, you'll discover where you can add the most value and how to thrive there. Yet, as with all organizations, you may discover things that don't work for you; and perhaps you'll figure out a way to improve upon them.

It's best to speak your truth as an observation and then follow up with a solution.

For instance, you may disagree with a lot of your company's policies. Vocalizing your concerns in a nonconstructive way will just put you further and further outside the circle—and highlight your sense of being a fish out of water. It's better to speak your truth as an observation and then follow that up with a solution. Otherwise, your negative comments will be perceived as downright irritating. If you fall into this category, you know who you are! Just watch coworkers' eyes glaze over when your hand goes up.

Showing that you are a fan means becoming your own fan, first. It means staying positive, finding solutions, dedicating yourself to the endgame, not giving up when things get tough, and believing in yourself. It's a tall order for those who have always had a comfortable life. It's a game played best by fish out of water—those of us who never had it easy in the first place. We're used to busting through walls and ceilings to make it in this world. Celebrate all those accomplishments and you'll find your inner fan to cheerlead your own success and the success of those around you.

Step 3 Exercises

Being fearless means never swimming alone in rough seas.

List three key people inside your company or industry who make you feel comfortable.

1. _____
2. _____
3. _____

From the list below, circle all of your passions:

Skiing	Hiking	Baseball	Biking
Cooking	Traveling	Performing	Speaking

Politics	Green Causes	Animals	Children
Nature	Dancing	Art	Gardening
Music	Reading	Movies	Television

Others

_____

How can you bring these people and passions into your work life?

_____

_____

Ideally, what characteristics do I want my coworkers, bosses, and/or customers to possess?

Integrity	Fairness	Tolerance	Diversity
Safety	Caring	Compassion	Aggressiveness
Positive Attitude	Generosity	Creativity	Authenticity
Hip/Cool	Green	Selective	Humor
Talent	Cutting Edge	Professional	Experience
Eagerness	Enthusiasm	Risk Taker	Collaborative

Others

_____

List your mentors and/or role models. Describe why you admire them.

1. _____
   _____
   _____

2. _____
   _____
   _____

3. _____
   _____
   _____

Identify a few people whom you would like to mentor you (business coaches count, too!)

1. _____
2. _____
3. _____

Describe your strategy for successfully creating a mentoring relationship with one of these people.

_____
_____
_____

List those people whom you'd like to mentor and why.

1. _____
2. _____
3. _____

Describe your strategy for successfully mentoring these people.

_____

_____

_____

_____

_____

_____

_____

_____

_____

Step 4

Swim in Their Ocean
Your Way

Fearless Fish Out of Water Find Ways
to Adopt the Company Culture
Without Getting Sucked In

- Be a cultural detective.
- Hold onto your style.
- Know when it's time to go.

Every time I take on a new client, I enter a new corporate culture. I am in every way myself, but I adapt slightly, as needed, to encourage connection and enhance a sense of familiarity. To start, I look for what interests me in the culture and then I pursue those interests. For example, it's been many years since I attended an Alabama football game, but I've never forgotten the thrill. So when it came time to take on CSTV (the college sports network) as a client, I could get behind the brand and write copy like a fan. I just focused on what I knew and loved about the experience to fit right in with the upbeat culture.

Once, when I was talking about the glory days of Alabama football with the CEO, he asked me where I had gone to high school, it seemed to him that I couldn't possibly be from the South. When I told him Beachwood High outside of Cleveland, he said he'd grown up in Shaker Heights, an adjacent suburb. It turned out that my first real boyfriend was now his brother-in-law! An incredible connection.

On the other end of the client spectrum is Southern California Edison. Not surprisingly, the electric company has a very professional and conservative corporate culture completely different from a television network like

CSTV. To become familiar with each other, we started our relationship with a classic business lunch. I asked questions about the lives of my new clients, their children and past work experiences, and then just listened intently to the answers. I found out that we all shared a passion for international travel, that we all were parents, and that the head of the department had lived in Atlanta as I once had.

These connections created a bond and provided insight into their company culture. Although we may have looked like we were from different worlds on the outside, on the inside, we all were adventurous and spirited people who put family first.

And that's what happens. The further you go to create connections, the more you can uncover where you fit in and find comfort in the culture.

Being a square peg trying to force your way into a round hole can affect both your professional *and* personal life long-term.

Step 4 in becoming a Fearless Fish out of water is all about learning how to be a part of almost any culture without getting lost in it. It can be deadly to get so entrenched that you can't find the real you. Fitting in to such a degree stifles creativity for people who are different—especially if the corporate environment is monotone. The job becomes just that—a job. Being a square peg trying to force your way into a round hole can affect both your professional *and* personal life long-term. Starting turf wars, becoming cynical, gossiping, finding scapegoats, and seeking to jump ship are just some of the psychological behaviors people fall back on when they feel forced to play along.

I know from my own experience that I would retreat to these behaviors when working for bosses who wanted me to wear a "corporate hat." On some level, it became more comfortable to blame others for my frustrations at work than to look inward to see if my unrealistic need for perfection and drive for more control was to blame.

If your organization has more than 10 people in it, chances are there is a robust political atmosphere: There are cliques, judgments, history, factions, embedded processes, good guys and bad guys, and so forth. When you're on the outside, it's up to you to find what's positive in the situation, what works for you, and to direct your attention there. When you focus on what you groove with, you'll be heading inside *your* way. But remember: You're interested in belonging through authenticity not conformity. What will be a tremendous help to you is putting on your deerstalker hat and becoming like Sherlock Holmes.

Be a cultural detective. Your detective work can begin before your first day of work. The Internet is a gold mine of information. Visit the company's web site, study its mission statement, read about its vision, check the list of 100 Best Corporate Citizens to see if it is on it, and whether the company's approach to business is aligned with yours. When you start a new job, locate the company historian, the one who's been there for years. Take that person to lunch and ask questions about the company, its policies, its culture, and others who've been there for a long time. Explain that you want to make a difference, you want to have an effect, and ask for advice. Who in the company—either historically or recently—has made a positive difference and/or a significant contribution?

Your initiative to become vested in the company will become a beacon to others.

Conversely, give that person some insight into who you are. Describe how the company's vision and mission inspire you, and share your idea about the synergy you and the company can create. Your initiative to become vested in the company will become a beacon to others—all because you're a fish out of water creating the environment you want to swim in.

Your conversation can build an alliance, one that strengthens your understanding of how to operate effectively and create positive impressions. That's what Kenetta Bailey, senior vice president of marketing at WEtv did when she joined the network. She came from Kraft Foods and sought out Todd Greene, vice president of affiliate marketing, because she heard he was a rising star who had worked in packaged goods. They could speak the same language and that created a comfort zone for her to talk with him about what she needed to do in order to fit into the culture and get things done.

Devote yourself to embracing aspects of the culture that resonate with who you are.

Once you've connected with that person, file the information away in your memory bank under "company culture" and devote yourself to embracing aspects of the culture that resonate with who you are. What excites you? What drives you? If you are working for a company that is strong on philanthropy and you're someone who volunteers, play it up, and ask others to join in. If the company is a good corporate citizen, be one yourself. If your industry values diversity, make your next hire someone who is different from the rest of your staff. You are part of the culture— you help it stay strong, and you help it evolve.

Being a cultural detective is essential when it comes to being able to make an informed choice for yourself and your career.

Being a cultural detective is essential when it comes to being able to make an informed choice for yourself and your career. There's a fine line between fitting in and getting sucked in or overwhelmed by a company and its culture. Doing your homework will provide you with the clarity and perspective needed to determine if you and the company are a fit—even before you're hired. Once you're on the inside, it's a matter of being who you are. To do that, you need to maintain your authenticity to sustain a long and fruitful career.

In Step 1, you met David, a friend of mine who had driven limousines in San Diego. Prior to that job (which he took to make ends meet), he was hired by a well-known person in the self-empowerment field to head his creative department. For him to land the job, he had to do his homework and once he was hired, he had to seriously maintain to sustain.

I knew very little about this person, except what I'd seen of him on his television infomercials. I wasn't sure what he actually did or what his company produced. To get an insider's perspective on the company, I decided the best approach was to interview my friend's wife, who worked in the creative department. Perhaps she could shed light before my first meeting with the president.

She filled me in on what type of person the president was, the kind of relationship I'd be expected to have with him, what the cultural climate was like, the person I'd be directly reporting to, what skill sets the position required, and why she felt I'd be the right person for the job. The list of necessary skill sets required was daunting—five pages long. Turned out, there was only one thing I'd not done on that list: run a teleprompter. Because I am computer savvy and can type 130 words a minute, running a teleprompter was going to be a no-brainer.

But what really appeared to be an obstacle for me was figuring out how to work with the president. He was quite demanding and tended to operate in a stream-of-consciousness mode when it came to strategizing and getting creative. Could I work like that? Me, this organized, everything-in-its-place, logic-and-order, disciplined guy?

I was given the president's best-selling book as a gift. I took it home and began reading through it. As a writer, my assessment was that it wasn't well-written, but it had a compelling aspect to it that was very engaging. It struck me, "Has anyone taken this guy's work and organized it so that anyone can grasp the gist of it in an easy-to-read overview?"

I was sparked and immediately began working on creating a condensed and concise logic model of his work. A day later, I e-mailed my work to the department head. She loved it. We then set up a time the following week for me to interview with the president and a few other key people in the company.

A week later, I arrived at the company's headquarters, unaware that the interview would last seven-and-a-half hours. The last person I met with was the president. I was driven up to his estate and left in this huge baronial living room by myself. I sat on the couch waiting calmly.

Then the president came striding in. We shook hands and my interview with him commenced.

He started out by exclaiming, "No one has ever done anything like this for me. This is outstanding! If this is an example of what you produce, you're hired." Well, I accepted the job right then and there and reported for work the following Monday morning.

I would never have been offered that position if I'd not done my research into the president and his company. Once on the job, I was able to continually impress him and others with my work and skill sets, though I also realized I had to loosen up some to really fit in.

It was quite a ride working for him and I learned a lot. I'm also proud of what I created and the impression I left on the staff. What's really important is that I never lost sight of myself in the process. I was able to maintain my strengths in skill sets and character, yet, at the same time, effectively work within their environment, expand my capabilities, and find a rewarding place for myself.

Being a cultural detective can actually be a lot of fun. It's a journey of discovery about the people and the environment and a chance for you to really figure out just how you feel about the company. As you start putting the pieces together, you're going to have various reactions to what you discover. Does what you're finding resonate with you? What differences and commonalities have you uncovered? What has surprised you in a good way and what has disappointed you? Who looks at things the way that you do? Where do you see a void that you are just the person to fill?

See your expedition as an adventure.

Like any good detective, you're piecing together a puzzle, one that, when completed, will create a direct connection between who you are, your skill sets, your sense of purpose, and the mission and vision of your company. See your expedition as an adventure, one that can only benefit you and your company, and you'll find that the decisions you make and the path you're on that much more rewarding.

Hold onto your style. Giving up your look can be like giving up your soul. The same is true for your personality. When you change so much for others that you can't recognize yourself in the mirror, it can be pretty scary.

Back when I had IBM as a client, literally every person there wore a blue, button-down shirt and had the demeanor of an ex-jock. In fact, for most of the twentieth century, the uniform for IBM employees was a dark (or gray) suit, white shirt (or the rebellious blue), and a "sincere" tie.

Toward the end of my tenure as a consultant to their Internet sports marketing division (where we developed web sites for franchises like the NHL and PGA), CEO Lou Gerstner relaxed the dress code so that IBM employees resembled their counterparts in other large technology companies.

With that change (and so many others implemented by Gerstner that literally saved the company from going out of business), IBM's relevance and revenues raced forward into the new millennium. IBM may still be known as "Big Blue," but the corporate uniform and rigid, insular culture of its mainframe computer company days has definitely shifted with its move to being an information technology integrator. Today, IBM's culture encourages individuality, which is expressed in dress and thinking. This, I believe, goes hand in hand with—and goes a long way toward—creating a culture where people feel respected, appreciated, and valued for who they are.

It's important to figure out what works for you in your company's cultural climate.

It's important to figure out what works for you in your company's cultural climate and dress code and what doesn't, and then adopting—and adapting—what fits for you. While at college, I learned many lessons on this subject that helped me immensely after graduation.

I'll never forget the first time I went to watch the Alabama Crimson Tide play football. The morning of game day, I left my dorm and arrived at the sorority house dressed in denim shorts, t-shirt, and Converse sneakers. Like most girls in the Greek system at "Bama," I had a date coming to pick me up for the game.

I walked upstairs and peeked in the bathroom. My new sisters were buzzing with excitement; putting on makeup, swapping dresses, and pulling hot rollers out of their hair. All at once one of the actives looked at me and with swift authority sent the order out to get me a dress and heeled sandals. Whoa! It was about 110 degrees outside and from my experience going to Ohio State games, I was perfectly dressed. But, I was in a different culture.

After putting on the dress I felt best reflected me— the one without a repeating pattern of spouting whales or pineapples, I went down to the front door to greet my date who to my amazement had on a navy blazer, white button-down shirt, striped tie, khaki pants, and penny loafers. Looking out beyond him, I saw a sea of boys dressed exactly like him standing at other sorority houses getting ready to pick up their dates.

> *To add to the initial shock, my date presented me with a corsage in a clear plastic box. It was a bright yellow mum the size of King Kong's fist adorned with a red pipe cleaner twisted into a letter "A" with a dangling gold football. He asked me if he could pin it on my dress. I went along with it because I hated the idea of disappointing this well-mannered, well-meaning Southern gentleman.*
>
> *Out of respect for Bear Bryant, the greatest college football coach in history, and the school's culture and traditions, for the next four years I wore dresses or skirts to football games, but I did it with my own flair, and I asked every one of my dates to please refrain from bringing me a corsage.*

At the University of Alabama, there was prejudice I disagreed with and a dress code as unfamiliar to me as the accent. I was out of my element. But I was determined to make it because there was a warmth and aliveness that drew me in and made me feel grounded. So I looked for what made me happy, what resonated with my soul. Right away, I knew I liked Southern food and Southern hospitality, and as time went on, I found I enjoyed the popular "beach" music, the classic traditions, and antebellum architecture. Before long, I was an expert at sucking down oysters, eating boiled peanuts, and a big fan of swing dancing. I didn't buy into the racism or trade in my cutoffs for plaid Bermuda shorts; I chose what worked for me and had the time of my life.

Safia K. Rizvi, senior director of influenza franchise marketing, GlaxoSmithKline, literally was transported from one culture to a completely new and different culture halfway around the world. She truly felt like a fish out of her element, floundering in a sea of tremendous differences. But with courage and her resolve to remain true to herself, she became a Fearless Fish out of water.

At age 21, I arrived in Oklahoma from Karachi, Pakistan. A recruiter had come to Pakistan representing a coalition of schools. The actual interview occurred in Southeast Asia. I was offered a scholarship to earn a master's degree in business at one of 13 different schools in the United States.

My parents were so against this. They wanted me to get married and become a wife—something traditional. I wanted more. So, I snuck behind my parents' backs to fill out the applications and sent them to all the schools. It turns out that there was a professor from Pakistan at the University of Oklahoma. He helped me by writing to my father and actually speaking with him. It took a lot of persuasion to convince both my parents.

When I arrived at the University of Oklahoma, I felt like a complete fish out of water at the business school—I had a Ph.D. in chemistry. I had no idea about demand and supply curves. One of my classmates mentioned a leveraged buyout. I had to ask her twice to explain what that was. I just didn't know the terminology.

I had to actually train my brain to think a different way. In science, you have a narrow subject and study it in depth. In business, you have broad information and you have to make decisions in a short time. Scientists don't open their mouths until they are 120 percent sure of their decisions. At business school, I couldn't learn everything in detail. I had to go more with my gut, rather than considering and analyzing all the possible data.

I really struggled and had to change the way I think. Of course, this brought up self-esteem issues, but, as usual, I worked to remain who I am in spite of my challenges. For instance, I don't have a very corporate *appearance. I've been told to cut my hair shorter to appear more businesslike. I wear my hair in a very long, traditional braid. But, you know, this is me. I'm attached to my hair not only physically, but emotionally. I don't want to have to change who I am to achieve success. I want to be successful as me.*

It helped to surround myself with people who care and who are smart; people who look for the good in everyone and get the best out of you.

In order to feel comfortable in their place of work or community, many people like to surround themselves with others who reflect their values, beliefs, and looks. Ever watch how people will stare at someone who appears out of the ordinary? What they're doing is evaluating the person by how he looks and acts. Does the person fit into my world and how do I feel about him? It's related to that old adage about fearing what we don't know or immediately understand. So, the question for you is: What are you going to do about it?

Do your homework and hold onto your style.

And the answer is: Do your homework and hold onto your style. Once people get to know you, they'll appreciate your being a fish out of water and realize what a valuable asset you are to them as a person and as a colleague in the company. You'll find your stride by determining what to hold onto and what you can either let go of or modify—without losing yourself in the process. Again, it's about adopting and adapting to the culture you find yourself in.

It's always interesting to watch how politicians adopt the culture they find themselves in. Whether they are at a fried chicken fund-raiser, a meeting of blue-collar workers or a black-tie event surrounded by Hollywood celebrities, they are always adopting the appropriate style to fit the room. In recent memory, no one did it better than President Bill Clinton—a man who could fit in anywhere and talk to anyone. Perhaps it was because at his core he wanted so badly to be liked. That's the motivation for many of us, but not all of us are as adept at small talk or can change up our style so drastically to blend in. For you, the fish out of water, that's where it all becomes problematic.

The fearless people I talk about in this book keep looking for the way in and adjust their conduct or approach, but never change their character. How do you show your style? If it isn't an honest expression, if it feels stifled or false trying to blend in, it's time for some new ideas. It's time either to tailor your style to your company's culture without completely selling out or to find a new company or create a company that embraces the real you.

Of course, this implies change, a word that scares a lot of people. What a lot of people forget is that they've already been through all sorts of changes in their lives and they're still here, thriving and full of life. We fish out of water are definitely accustomed to this; yet, at times, we forget or are overwhelmed by what we're faced with and run or hide. But then we resurface, and remember that change is our friend not our enemy.

Change is something to look forward to and not something to hide from.

Change is something to look forward to and not something to hide from. I've never known change not to be for the better. Even when it's challenging, change forces you to look at yourself and decide what you really want. Change keeps you from growing complacent and getting stuck. It's a chance to reinvent oneself or explore new territory. Every time I've left a relationship, a position, or the city I live in, it's been a positive experience. It may not always be your choice, but it will almost always be for the best.

When change occurs, you have to stick to your style, your core identifiers.

When change occurs, you have to stick to your style, your core identifiers. When times get tough, look back at your track record and identify how your own individual style helped you succeed in life. Then, let it be a touchstone to get you through unfamiliar territory, *fearlessly*. As Graciela Meibar says, "You have to be authentic. You have to accommodate to some degree the overall culture, but never stop being who you are. If you are not authentic to who you are, or pretend or please, you lose who you are."

Know when it's time to go. Now and then, no matter how you try, the shoe just doesn't fit—you simply cannot get inside and embrace the culture. If this is true, it could be time to say "thank you" and move on.

How do you know when it's time to seek greener pastures? My own experience of not being able to embrace the culture of a start-up media company taught me about the importance of having values in alignment with your coworkers.

> *A few years ago, my company was hired to create a brand strategy and marketing plan for a new venture backed by former Kiss front man Gene Simmons. The project entailed launching a television network and web site that*

featured uncensored music videos. At first, I was excited. I had loved being part of the music business as a concert promoter in college and as a marketing manager at a record store chain and pop radio station.

Sadly, however, Gene's company was like a fabulously dysfunctional family. Toilet humor was constant, and sexual innuendo and derogatory comments marked the men's exchanges with me and with each other. I could tell right away this wasn't a match—I was off my path, walking down memory lane instead of striding boldly into my future. I was out of my depth—meaning that I was out of the type of environment that truly worked for me.

I decided to quit. I agonized over the loss of revenue (which was significant). I concluded that no amount of money was enough for me to sell my soul. When I left, I gave the company copresidents hand-selected gifts that had special significance to them. They were stunned by my announcement and by my offerings, and I walked away committed to only pursuing work that is in alignment with who I am.

Sometimes, we have to have the courage to disappoint people when the culture isn't a fit.

That is one of the marks of the Fearless Fish: Know when to bow out gracefully. It could mean leaving money on the table or moving to another location entirely; sometimes, we have to have the courage to disappoint people when the culture isn't a fit. The hardest thing to do is to not take this type of situation personally; you mustn't see yourself as a failure, as having failed, or as having disappointed someone else. Beating ourselves up with blame for what went wrong is really egotistical when you stop and think about the fact that you were not the only one in the relationship. It's about seeing the positive beyond the situation.

Leaving a negative situation with grace, not burning bridges, showing appreciation (authentically and where appropriate), not getting into the blame game, or lost in details and gossip is the hallmark of someone who is growing and learning. The alternative just breeds bitterness and self doubt.

Linda is a marketing executive and a Fearless Fish who came to the conclusion that there wasn't a fit with her employer. She worked for one of the first video distribution sites on the Internet.

> *At 44 years of age, Linda moved to Los Angeles from Dallas to work in the entertainment industry. She was a cultural fish out of water from the start. But her job turned out to be even more of a mismatch.*
>
> *Linda is a serious businessperson, and she was the only woman in upper management among a group of young hipsters. From the start, it was clear to her that she was more concerned about the business than the rest of the staff. Everyone, including the CEO, went clubbing frequently after work, and there was pressure to stay out most of the night.*
>
> *At first, Linda tried to embrace this culture. But after a couple of months, she stopped going out with her co-workers. She started getting the cold shoulder and soon found she wasn't being invited to meetings.*

There wasn't one aspect of the culture she could embrace, and on top of it, the money she felt was needed for her department's budget wasn't being allocated. Linda gave notice. Within a week, she received three good job offers.

Staying true to herself meant leaving her job without another in place, and the universe responded with help.

How good a fit are you with the culture of your workplace? Do you and your boss click or is working for your company becoming a demoralizing experience to the point where you are questioning your own abilities, capabilities, and perceptions? Is your head throbbing at the end of each day from hitting it against the wall? Is every suggestion you make at work met with an eye roll, or worse, a patronizing response? Is there racism, sexism, ageism, or a lack of acceptance because you look or sound different? Are you being sexually harassed or completely ignored? Perhaps your creative approach is 180 degrees in opposition to your colleagues; for example, you are thoughtful and let things percolate, whereas your colleagues are operating at the speed of light. You may be determined to stay on board and have the kind of work ethic that stops at nothing, but at what price?

You were born to reach your potential and live your destiny.

There are many reasons why a job isn't a fit. What it comes down to, essentially, is how you feel about yourself at the end of the day. You weren't born to be abused, you were born to reach your potential and live your destiny. When you're a fish out of water, it's easy to feel people just don't *get* you. But, if being different from everyone is not going to work where you are, you alone have the power to change your job. A good exit plan may be what you need if you find the effort is not worth the return.

Deciding to terminate your stint with a company can create a lot of anxiety. Are you doing the right thing? Did you give it your all? How are your colleagues going to take the news of your leaving? Will they try to stop you or get defensive and treat you like a traitor? Will you be able to find another job—especially one that really supports who you are?

All of these are valid questions and will require some introspection to figure out the answers. Here's what happened to my friend David, the one who worked for the self-empowerment guy covered earlier in this step.

My position as director of the creative department required I work between 80 to 100 hours per week, yet I only got paid for 40 hours. I found myself constantly filled with anxiety, wondering if I could get my workload accomplished, done well, and done on time. I consistently fell behind in some areas, but had no choice as I had to prioritize my workload. At the time, I only had two assistants who were working just as feverishly as I was.

The day came, though, when my body helped me make the decision to leave. I was at home, preparing to go in to work on a Saturday morning. As I walked from my kitchen around the corner toward my bedroom, I suddenly had a grand mal seizure (I have diabetes). I was not able to control myself and ended up scraping my face down the side of my apartment's heating unit, which is about five feet in height. I was out for the count.

Two hours later, I awoke, freezing cold and my face stuck to the carpet from the blood. I freaked out, managed to unglue myself from the carpet, stumbled into the bathroom, and looked at my face. I was a mess—and scared. I'd had seizures before, but never had I hurt myself. And, even worse—I was living alone at the time.

I cleaned myself up and needless to say, didn't go in to work that day. Instead, I made some hot tea and sat down to think, realizing I'd reached a dangerous crossroad concerning my place of business. The answer was more than clear that I couldn't stay there anymore. I'd delivered myself a two-by-four to the head.

Along with how this job was impacting my health, I realized that there was much more to think about. How was I being treated at work? Even though I put in an incredible amount of time meeting the president's demands, I was told by coworkers I wasn't a team player, because I wasn't living my life completely for the president. Instead of joyfully taking on more and more work, I was trying to protect myself and my staff to create a better working environment. I was standing up to the president instead of just immediately asking how high when he said, "Jump."

What I had come to realize finally is that I was in an abusive work relationship. And it was time I left.

That next Monday morning, I phoned in to tell my lead assistant about the seizure and that I wouldn't be coming in to work that day—and that I would be resigning at the end of the month. I'd stay only to help her and my other assistant long distance through the major seminar happening in one week in Hawaii, but then I was out of there.

The relief I felt was huge. I was so swept up in the company I'd lost sight of myself. I hadn't realized how *heavy of a load I'd been carrying for so long, that I'd compromised myself to the detriment of my health and well-being.*

Several months later, after having left the company, I had to go back to pick up something. My lead assistant, now director of that department took one look at me and said, "You look so much healthier and more at peace." That's all I needed to hear.

David's wake-up call was rather dramatic. Hopefully, most of us will bypass the drama and get the message much earlier. If, on the other hand, you simply need a new approach for embracing the culture, then follow the wisdom of other Fearless Fish who are swimming with the current. They've mastered the art of being a Fearless Fish out of water. Just as we've covered in each step, it's all about you. You need to go fishing for the real you, use your differences as a lure, find a few fish like you, and then learn to swim in their ocean *your* way.

As with most things in life, there's an appropriate time to be the rebel and times when you need to give the rebel a rest.

Now, before we move on to the exercises for this step, there's one thing we haven't covered: What if you have to swim against the current? Let's face it, for Fearless Fish, swimming against the current has been something we've done most of our lives. It has the patina of being a rebel. Sometimes it's been comfortable and even fun. Other times, it's meant weathering rough waters. As with most things in life, there's an appropriate time to be the rebel and times when you need to give the rebel a rest.

It can be difficult to determine when swimming upstream is the best decision for you. It comes down to, again, doing what's best for you and *that which supports you*. If you're being a rebel simply for the sake of being a rebel, then you've probably got a chip on your shoulder—which is actually about lack of self-esteem. *If the world isn't going to give me the respect I deserve, then I'm going to make 'em deal with me!* Not exactly a winning strategy. What will most likely happen is that you'll not get respect, but instead get the lack of respect you perceived you were getting in the first place. You'll have self-sabotaged the situation.

On the other hand, if swimming against the current involves maintaining respect for the company culture and supports and complements your company's mission, then get vocal. Sometimes, it means pointing out painful things about the company—as long as you have solutions to offer that are still in alignment with the company's focus and product and not about self-aggrandizement.

Whatever the reasons are for your deciding to swim against the current, be sure of your reasons for doing so.

There may be times when swimming against the current is about helping companies get back on track because they've become distracted. Perhaps the company needs a new "big picture" to work with or it needs to get itself in fighting shape because it's become top heavy. You may see something coming down the pike that the company is oblivious to, something that could be either highly damaging or incredibly transforming. And then there are times when you might go against the grain simply to prove yourself. Whatever the reasons are for your deciding to swim against the current, be sure of your reasons for doing so.

Susan O'Meara, the American filmmaker living in Ireland you read about in Step 3, definitely swam against the current as she tried not only to fit in, but to figure out who she was.

> *Frankly, I wasn't brave enough to forge my own way. I always thought courage was about the big things, the big risk, like rescuing a kid off the tracks as an oncoming train hurtles down the railway. But I see now it's in the small, daily things about which we refuse to compromise ourselves.*
>
> *Corporate culture just rubbed me fundamentally the wrong way. Sure, I tried my best; but my feelings got the better of me and my emotions would be written all over my face. I couldn't play the game. I had no interest in it and I thought it was a waste of time, energy, creativity, and common sense. Speak your mind and get on with it—that wasn't encouraged. I guess the overriding questions are: How to fit in without losing yourself? Or how to set yourself apart without losing your (1) bosses, (2) peers, and (3) career momentum?*
>
> *In order to be your true-blue self, to love and live that about yourself, I think you have to embody the Scarlett O'Hara stance of not giving a damn what others believe about you. Your journey is your own; no one else walks in your slippers or loafers or Blahniks.*
>
> *I suppose it's backward in a way, but I often relish being underestimated. It actually strikes me as kind of funny, even hilarious. Someone's blasé "Oh, really?," or condescending, "You think so?" doesn't seem so much a challenge as a boost to my confidence. "You'll see," I say to*

myself (and if you don't, that's your problem). I relax into myself and take on the project or challenge with quiet gusto. It's fun to prove people wrong by virtue of not so much proving yourself, as just being yourself.

Leaving the Showtime Networks fold in 1988 set me free in ways I never could have imagined. One morning, on my way into work on Manhattan's No. 1 subway, I knew I had to make my getaway. Immediately! I had no plan and even fewer savings, but I just couldn't breathe anymore. I walked into my boss's office and said: "I have to leave." "Do you have an appointment or something?" "No, I mean for good."

This caused some minor chaos, but within a month, I'd extricated myself and become a consultant for the very same company—at twice the pay grade. One of the best moves I've ever, ever made.

Swimming upstream, as Susan did, turned out to be the best move for her. Though she'd developed some wonderful friendships with her colleagues, what was more important to her was finding the place where she fit—in spite of what others were telling her or what the accepted career course was. Swimming against the current meant being herself, eventually realizing that Showtime Networks wasn't for her and then moving on with her life.

For you, fish out of water that you are, you are now coming into your own. Learning to swim in their ocean your way is not only about supporting yourself, it's about carpe diem—seizing the day—and making it your own. You have it all within you. Now you just need to let it out and truly become the Fearless Fish out of water.

Step 4 Exercises

Whoever said you had to be like everyone else didn't have a clue.

What is the company culture like in your industry or organization? (Research the company's web site.)

_____

_____

_____

After doing your research, what do you think you can bring to the company?

_____

_____

_____

Who is the company historian? How can you gain knowledge from that person? What questions would you ask?

_____

_____

_____

_____

How do you show your style? In the way you dress and act? In other ways?

_____

_____

_____

_____

_____

Do you successfully blend in or do you feel stifled or inauthentic?

_____

_____

_____

How can you stay true to your company's culture while staying true to yourself?

_____

_____

_____

Here are some questions to determine if it's time to leave your current position. Answer yes or no to all of them. If you've answered yes to more than two, it's probably time to plan a graceful exit strategy.

____ Is the culture of your workplace a difficult fit for you?

____ Does your boss put you down or pass you over for promotions?

____ Is your job a demoralizing experience?

____ Do you question your own abilities, capabilities, and/or perceptions?

____ Is your head throbbing at the end of each day from hitting it against the wall?

____ Are your suggestions met with a patronizing response?

___ Is there racism, sexism, ageism, or a lack of acceptance because you look or sound different?

___ Are you being sexually harassed or completely ignored?

Other_____

_____

_____

How will you leave your current position gracefully and with integrity?

_____

_____

_____

_____

_____

_____

If you've made the choice to stay, how will you change to make it work?

_____

_____

_____

_____

_____

_____

Step

Put Yourself Out on the Line

Fearless Fish Out of Water Are Natural Advocates Because They See the World Through a Different Lens

- Advocate for yourself.
- Advocate for others.
- Advocate for a greater good.
- Advertise your accomplishments.

Every January, I make a fix-it checklist. At the start of 2007, I noted that during the work week, I only shared two hours a day with my seven-year-old daughter. That was not tolerable to me. My health was also at the top of the list; migraines and other stress-related disorders had begun to take their toll on me. The balance of the list was concerns about L.A. traffic and air quality, safety issues, my work, and my time. I clearly needed to make a dramatic shift.

My husband and I hired Steve Shull, an L.A.-based business coach, to help us reprioritize our lives to find more joy, peace, and balance. By shining a light on the things that needed to be fixed, the solutions became clear. By the end of 2007, we moved to Santa Fe, New Mexico; hired someone to run our New York office; empowered the people in our L.A. office; and cut the cord. A week or two after we arrived in our new home and started spending more time with our daughter, business started rolling in—a validation of my favorite truism, "change is good."

Remember, change is our friend, not our enemy.

Fearless Fish out of water are nonconformists who are good at taking the bull by the horns and creating positive change for themselves. We recognize that change is our friend, not our enemy. Even though we may understand that concept intellectually, we may need a little nudge to prompt us to take action. But when we do—look out! As with all change, we have to take a risk and put ourselves out on the line. That's another facet of what makes Fearless Fish different from others: We'll go out on a limb, we'll stick our necks out, we'll step off a cliff into thin air; we trust ourselves! And this works wonders for the world around us.

The ones who are different are perfectly positioned to *make* a difference.

Those who are different are perfectly positioned to *make* a difference. It's not the wallflower who's going to help a company go green, or the conformist who will invent the new business model or product. As a fish out of water, you can create change—and be an inspiration—because you *don't* blend in, you *do* get noticed, and when you put the tools for being a Fearless Fish into practice, you'll also be heard.

Nathalie Lubensky of Disney and ESPN Media Networks has turned her success into a means of advocating for others.

> *I'm acting as an agent for change by looking at everyone's opportunities and figuring out how to help them. I feel like I fell into this profession to make work easier for me and to make it more fulfilling for others. I'm looking to see how I can affect people's lives. Mentoring others, getting people promoted—it's all part of trying to make it easier so no one feels like a fish out of water.*

As a fish out of water, your most apparent gift is being just that. Nathalie—and many of the people I've introduced you to in this book—made this most important discovery about themselves. You're in the same position. Recognition is the beginning. Learning to use your differences as a lure; finding others like you; and learning to adapt and adopt within a company using your fish-out-of-water uniqueness are all about positioning yourself for the next step: advocacy.

It's all about being proactive instead of settling.

Step 5 to becoming a Fearless Fish out of water challenges you to learn to use your differences to everyone's advantage by advocating for yourself and for others. It's all about being pro-active instead of settling. Fish out of water can become so accustomed to discomfort they forget that it doesn't have to be that way. It's time to look beyond the problem to see what's possible and create whatever change is needed.

True advocacy happens at the nexus of integrity and inspiration. It takes your personal values, beliefs, creative ideas, and intent into consideration, and puts them side by side with your company's mission, vision, and initiatives. It doesn't impose anything on colleagues, but rather seeks to expand and sustain on a level that benefits everyone. It brings people and ideas together to cultivate a corporate "field of dreams."

News flash: Advocates that become self-righteous and obsessive can lose sight of their original intention. They also have a tendency to stop listening to everyone around them, which means creativity, imagination, expansiveness, resourcefulness, and flexibility are left in the dust.

So, let's look at true advocacy: advocating for yourself, advocating for others, advocating for a greater good, and advertising your accomplishments.

Advocate for yourself. It's up to you to create the life you want, and it takes discernment—knowing when it's time to make changes as you go after what you really want. After having completed the exercises in the previous steps, you probably have a clearer idea of what you want to go after. If you're still trying to figure that out, here's a way that will help you: Distinguish between what's working well for you as opposed to what you are just *tolerating* at home and at work. Maybe it's time to stop putting up with so much. There are two parts to this: The first is recognizing what isn't working, and the second is making appropriate changes.

To start, make a "fix-it checklist" like I do at the beginning of each year. To be clear—this is not a complaint list. It's sticking your flag in the ground and declaring, "This is happening, and it's got to change." It's making the need real, issuing a notice to yourself that life isn't just about tolerating things. It's about taking a positive stand for yourself and removing those things that are unacceptable. This could mean initiating a conversation with the boss to ask for solutions to your unbearably huge workload, or instituting a program for flextime. For me it was a sea change—a major life overhaul.

When the fix-it checklist is done, it's time to take action. Hiring a coach, as I did, or collaborating with a mentor can be invaluable. Results come quickly when your energy is focused and anchored by someone who is cheering you on. In only two months after making the move to Santa Fe, I saw a marked improvement in my health, my spirit, my marriage, and my relationship with my daughter. It all became a reality when my coach encouraged me to change my number one priority from my work to my health. Let's face it, without good health, you can't work! Now, every morning,

I ask myself what I'm going to do to keep my life in this order: (1) my health, (2) my husband, (3) my daughter, (4) my work, and (5) making the world a better place. From there, I prioritize the list of things I want to accomplish that day.

This method of directing focus works; it can be done during your commute or in the shower. The rewards are great when you discipline yourself to set an intention every day and visualize a positive outcome. Instead of feeling overwhelmed and flying off the handle, I set realistic goals and push everyone (including myself) with less force. Today, my daughter sees a mommy who isn't afraid of what might happen and instead is dealing with what is happening in the moment.

News flash: A bad economy doesn't give you an excuse to put your personal happiness on hold. You can walk around all day in fear or you can move forward with faith. The choice is yours. Standing strong in tough times is good role modeling for your children and for your inner child. You can learn who you really are in a crisis. This is the time to show yourself and everyone around you what you are made of. Be fearless in the storm and everyone in your personal and professional life will gravitate to your strength.

Sometimes the most effective change comes from changing our point of view.

Sometimes, what we're tolerating has to do with perception, and the most effective change comes from changing our point of view. For example, let's say you've put "crummy boss" at the top of your tolerance list. She's cranky, impatient, comes down hard on you and others for no apparent reason, and her demands of you are unreasonable. The solution? It could be that you need to apply for a transfer out of her department, or leave the company entirely. If you feel the need to bolt, let me suggest that before you do, consider whether your unhappiness could be a case of misperception. Maybe she's not a crummy boss. Maybe she's a pressured boss you could view differently. You could invite her out to lunch to get a sense of what's going on with her through a more personal exchange. Chances are she won't tell all, but if gently prodded, she may reveal something of her feelings about her job or her homelife. Maybe there's an ill mother-in-law crowding her at home, or a teenager she's anxious about or— like you—she has a boss that's coming down on her. If you can find the human connection, your perceptions may shift and your experience may improve along with it.

The human connection is key here. Though you are a fish out of water, as we covered in Step 4, you need to learn to swim in their waters while maintaining your personal integrity. The best way to make that happen is by connecting with people. The people around you may initially find you so different from them— maybe even scary—that it may be difficult to get to know them. But, if you follow the steps we've covered so far, you'll get past the initial phase of awkwardness, begin introductions, and develop relationships that create a supportive, win-win situation. Your sensitivity and consideration of other people will be recipro- cated—you, the fish out of water who takes the lead by modeling, then becomes the model leader. Once you're in that position, you can begin to become an advocate and make big changes.

However, if there's nothing there but bitterness or un- reasonable demands surrounding your situation—then move on fearlessly! That's what I did with a client recently. To advocate for myself and my company, I had to bow out of a project with an impossible timetable. Before we could even begin to meet the deadline, we had to receive artwork and copy from our client six weeks in advance. At four weeks to launch, we still had not received those essential assets. Our hands were tied. We knew from experience there was no way to have a successful outcome; so we called the managers on the project and asked that they find another agency to do the job. The next day, the company's head of marketing called to say she was personally disappointed in me. I had acted with integrity; but she was not impressed.

When you are advocating for yourself, not everyone is going to see your decisions as good for them. Sure, I could have tried to get the impossible done (that's what pleasers do); but if we missed the deadline or turned out subpar work, the consequences would have been more severe than a little disappointment.

At the end of the day, this is your life, and if it's not working, you've got to do something about it. If you have an abusive client, fire them. If your job is killing your soul and you've forgotten who you are, dump it. Don't wait to become vested in your 401k, or hope your boss is going to be fired, or hold your breath in the hopes that someone is going to finally recognize your talent and value. It's time to stop the magical thinking you do in the perfect world of your mind.

News flash: You've got to stand up for yourself, or you won't stand a chance. The only person who's going to appreciate your being a martyr is you. Meanwhile, the world is going to keep on rolling by unless you ground yourself in who you are—a unique fish out of water. Step up to the plate, grasp the bat of clarity firmly, and calmly set your sights on success—by advocating for yourself.

Advocate for others. People like Graciela Meibar and H Lewis are making a difference because they're creating change that contributes to the greater good. Graciela is one of the few top Hispanic female executives in the United States. She has started a lunch program for the women in her organization because she wants them to feel connected and empowered. She brings in speakers who spread the word about how to make the most of being a woman in business.

And what about H Lewis? He found the well-mannered Southern culture in Atlanta to be very consensus-driven. His colleagues could be very passive/aggressive because they felt they couldn't say in meetings what was on their minds. To open up communication, he facilitated a "Rock the Boat" and "Conflict Dynamics" training program to help people talk about how they feel; but he did it in a contextual way that's tied to the work and doesn't ruffle feathers. "Now when we want to get ideas out on the table, we do less self-editing so the business can be more innovative," he explains.

Contributing helps you increase your involvement, up your value, better your reputation, and inspire trust.

H and Graciela prove that contributing helps you increase your involvement and enhance your value. You better your reputation by inspiring trust. Helping others is also good for self-esteem; it feels good, and when you feel good, more creative juices flow.

Your greatest contribution could be helping other fish out of water.

Your greatest contribution could be helping other fish out of water. If you could help one person, who would it be? Are there others like you who need help as well? Is there something you can do inside your company that could benefit others? Take a stand and see what happens. You never know what doors may suddenly open for you.

Advocating for someone else does feel good. However, you have to make sure that you're doing it for the right reasons and not just caretaking. The key is to support what you stand for and serve your company's greater good. The clarity you have discovered about yourself must be applied to any coworker or colleague you choose to stand up for. Discuss all of that individual's ideas, accomplishments, and vision for the future as it pertains to your department and, therefore, the company. Ask questions and get a clear understanding of where this individual feels he fits into the company and what he has to offer. Determine where there is alignment and divergence, as both have their advantages and disadvantages.

Once you've completed your exploration, determine how you'd like to proceed. And make sure the person you're advocating for understands where you're coming from and why you choose to advocate for him. Whether you're advocating for an idea or for a person, clarity, honesty, and sincerity are the hallmarks of success.

News flash: It's important to look inside to make sure your motives are grounded. Though this may have the appearance of office politics, it really isn't about that at all. If your focus is about connecting in a genuine way, then your objective is for the greater good—something we'll be discussing next. If what you're advocating involves hidden agendas and political maneuverings to gain power, prestige, or control over others, then the people around you will pick up on that.

Being aware of both sides of the advocacy coin is important. Clearly understanding your role and your fellow workers' abilities and capacities will ensure the company's forward movement. It's all about doing your work in an inclusive and enthusiastic manner. If your head and heart are in the right place, you're ready for the next step: advocating for a greater good.

Advocate for a greater good. Digging deep to find the social advocate inside you and taking action to help others on a wider scale has far-reaching rewards.

Susan O'Meara, the filmmaker and documentarian now living in Ireland, combined her love of film, people, and causes and created a new business that brings cultures and good food to the rest of the world.

Just this year I started Pembroke Pictures or fun with film, as I like to call it. Along with my two partners, Cynthia Kane of ITVS and Deborah Goodwin of Franklin Street Independent Productions, we've been working on two documentary projects for the past three years. The first is By Bread Alone: In the Company of Food Heroes, *in which we follow home several astonishing food heroes from the "United Nations of food," Terra Madre (Mother Earth), sponsored by Slow Food International.*

We filmed the "heroes" initially in Turin, Italy, the home of Terra Madre in the autumn of 2006. It featured 5,000 delegates—farmers, fishermen, artisans—from 130 countries, many of whom have never been out of their own villages. These are people who struggle to feed their families, neighbors, and communities; they take to the sea and to the land to plant, grow, harvest, and share their life's work: healthy, safe, fair trade food that's good for the planet.

We plan to film a farming cooperative in Piedmonte, Italy; storm-ravaged New Orleans where half the restaurants and farmers' markets are still out of business; Chefs for Peace in Jerusalem; a cheese maker in the Republic of Ireland and a baker in Northern Ireland who've joined forces; and Alice Waters at Slow Food Nation in 2008. We're off to a great start!

One way to change negative impressions or stereotypes is to do good work—both on the job and out in the world.

Fish out of water often feel out of the mainstream because others tend to be uncomfortable with their differences. One way to change negative impressions or stereotypes is to do good work, both on the job and out in the world. When you connect in significant ways with the community, people see you differently; you become a leader for the greater good. And by rallying others for a good cause, you become more successful in life. It's instant karma. Here's what I mean:

After Hurricane Katrina hit New Orleans in August 2005, hotel owner Sidney Torres IV saw a need to clean up the growing mountains of garbage. Reinventing himself as a waste-management CEO, Torres bought a couple of garbage trucks, gave them a pristine black exterior and chrome wheels, branded them with his signature bull logo, and submitted the winning bid to collect garbage in New Orleans' French Quarter and beyond. The French Quarter has never been cleaner; a fact that's significantly bolstering its image. It's helping Torres' image, too. Last year, he was honored as grand marshal of the Mardi Gras parade.[1]

Bill Clinton is someone who increased his personal equity and relevance through his philanthropy. By doing good work to help poor nations, he shifted the focus from the scandal surrounding him to important issues and innovative solutions. Bill Gates changed public perception of himself in positive ways with

[1]Referenced at www.nola.com/living

his massive philanthropic contributions. Oprah is known for her generosity, as are U2's Bono and a number of other high profile celebrities who've increased their brand equity and career longevity through acting on their conscience.

Author and activist Ray Anderson is another person who has used his influence to advocate for the greater good. Ray is a world-renowned supporter of sustainable industry. In 1997, he was named cochair of the President's Council on Sustainable Development, and in 1999, he published a book titled *Mid-Course Correction: Toward a Sustainable Enterprise—The Interface Model* about his conversion to sustainability. Anderson's vision changed his company, Interface, Inc., and the petroleum-intensive industry of carpet manufacturing forever.

Ray experienced an epiphany after reading Paul Hawken's The Ecology of Commerce, *while he was seeking inspiration for a speech about the company's environmental vision. Fourteen years and a sea change later, Interface, Inc., is nearly 50 percent of the way toward attaining its vision of "Mission Zero," an initiative that promises to "eliminate any negative impact it may have on the environment, by the year 2020, through the redesign of processes and products, the pioneering of new technologies, and efforts to reduce or eliminate waste and harmful emissions, while increasing the use of renewable materials and sources of energy."*

Ray travels the world spreading awareness about sustainability with passion and intelligence. His goals are to uplift humanity and bring about a transformation of business and industry and raise the consciousness of coworkers about how to lead a sustainable life on Earth. At the same time, he commands the world's largest producer of commercial floor coverings. Interface has diversified and globalized its businesses with sales in 110 countries and manufacturing facilities on four continents.

Anderson has been applauded by government, environmental, and business groups. In 2007, Ray received the Purpose Prize from Civic Ventures—a think tank that generates ideas and invents programs to help society achieve the greatest return on its experiences. He was also presented with Auburn University's International Quality of Life Award. Ray is a master commentator on the Sundance Channel's Big Ideas for a Small Planet, *and was named one of* Time *magazine's Heroes of the Environment in 2007, with a similar honor from* Elle *magazine that same year.*

Some of the world's great companies have become increasingly socially responsible; they know people want to do business with corporations that are conscientious and current. Nike isn't only about athletic shoes and clothing; it's about advocating a strong body and a healthy lifestyle. Avon isn't just about makeup; it's motivated millions of women to raise money for a breast cancer cure through sponsored long-distance runs. From McDonald's to Microsoft to MTV, great brands create staying power by championing a cause. They leverage brand equity for a greater good so that the company endures in the hearts and minds of its loyal customers. And you can do it, too.

With a little bit of effort, you can make a big difference.

With a little bit of effort, you can make a big difference like Telemundo's Michelle Bella. She started a green initiative for

Latinos called "Viva Verde." Her vision received the attention of top management at the parent company, General Electric, and has become a major focus of Telemundo and *all* of the television networks owned by GE. With actions like these, you help yourself; you help people in the immediate circle around you; and you help your community at large.

When I started Big Fish many years ago, I made a decision to "leverage entertainment for a greater good." With this mission, I've been able to work with my clients to develop community outreach programs such as Nickelodeon's "Big Green Help," an environmental initiative for kids; CNN's "Your Choice, Your Voice," a high school-based election promotion; FSN's "Reading All-Stars" literacy campaign; The History Channel's "Save Our History," which raised money and awareness for the World War II Memorial; and Comedy Central's "Comedy RX," a hospital-based program promoting the healing power of laughter. As a director on the board of the Aquarium of the Pacific, I helped craft a brand strategy to raise awareness for the aquarium's efforts to bring to the forefront the fragile nature of our oceans and the need to protect the animals that live there.

People often fear that getting involved in volunteering or in other outreach work will be costly, because it will take time away from their core business. This does not have to be true. In fact, creating change can be a business booster. My commitment to empowering others, for example, attracts clients to my business— especially those who are seeking a way to reach consumers in a more meaningful way. Since writing my first book, *Make a Name for Yourself*, and speaking to and mentoring thousands of men and women, I've doubled Big Fish Marketing's profits. What does that mean to me personally? That my life isn't devoted solely to helping businesses boost their profits; it's also about helping them to be more responsible. This gives my company depth and longevity in a here-today-gone-tomorrow industry like advertising.

As an agent for change inside of a company, you can be seen as a leader for a cause that others care about deeply. You're making a difference, while capitalizing on the power of your company's brand and resources. Perceptions about you and your corporation can change as you make change. The only downside is that you are often an army of one, the upside is you have people to answer to other than yourself. That's exactly how it is for Kelliegh Dulany, vice president of public responsibility, in charge of overseeing prosocial initiatives for Comedy Central and Spike.

Internally, I've been an agent for change. The green issue in Comedy Central's "Address the Mess" connects with our staff. So many people come up to me and say how awesome it is, and they want to volunteer. I've become the eco-representative for the company. For example, when we moved our office, I sent out company-wide e-mails telling everyone what we were doing to make this move a positive one for the planet. They looked to me as the expert.

The downside of this position is the upside. I have to be my own boss, and I'm steering the ship and stepping on the gas. I have a boss who supports my efforts, but at the end of the day, I'm the one who has to get things done. Sometimes you want to be supported and not be in charge of everything. That's the by-product of being in a brand new position and department of one. But, I get to be the key decision maker. If I don't push the agenda, it doesn't happen. I get people to rally around my ideas by showing the benefits to everyone in the room. I have to enroll them, not dictate to them what they have to do. There's a little bit of a halo effect: Associate with this and you'll be perceived in a positive light.

> *From a career standpoint, I've reinvented myself; no question. But my job no longer directly connects to revenue. I have some fear that if my company cuts back, I'm gone. But I'm so much happier because I've brought another component to my resume that expands my appeal. I think I'm easier to work with now because I'm happier—and that's what matters. My last job was so draining; this is uplifting. It's more collaborative and has more integrity. There's no selling out.*

By advocating for the greater good, you may also discover something new about yourself, such as just how passionate, determined, and engaging you can be. Taking a stand can be a great way to stretch yourself and, at the same time, develop an even deeper sense of personal authenticity.

Kelliegh's comment, "There's no selling out," is an important point. Remaining true to yourself is the basis of authenticity, something we covered in Steps 1 and 2. Selling out is something all of us are aware of and many of us do from time to time. In business there's always that pressure to compromise, to either sink or swim. And we all need to survive; but at what cost? Are we truly finding a balance between people and ideas; or are we allowing ourselves to be compromised in order to stay in the game, keep our heads above water, and move up the corporate ladder?

As a fish out of water, you've probably struggled with trying to maintain personal integrity, while at the same time wanting to fit in. It's very easy to lose yourself when your desire to be a part of a group or company overtakes your inner desire to be who you are. The pressures of family, friends, peers, and coworkers are often very difficult to withstand. In spite of that, what it all comes down to is that you are in charge of your life. It's up to you to create your destiny.

What makes your heart sing? What makes you soar inside?

What makes your heart sing? What makes you soar inside? What makes you feel like the world is your oyster and that anything is possible? Is it listening to music, working with children, dancing around the house, white-water rafting, being of service, building things, designing interiors, singing, writing, racing, producing events, or creating possibilities for others to achieve beyond their wildest dreams?

Once people see and experience your passion, great possibilities come into play.

Whatever quickens your heart and stimulates your mind, that's what you want to gravitate toward. Surround yourself with the people who are just as passionate about the same idea, concept, topic, philosophy, process, game, product, issue, or challenge as you—all within your company or organization. Once people see and experience your passion, great possibilities come into play. And when you've achieved your outcome, you need to let people know about it. Give others credit where credit is due, and highlight the accomplishments. Suddenly, you're more visible, seen as someone who makes things happen for the good of the company, the greater good of your community, and beyond.

Humility has its place, but so does recognizing and sharing your accomplishments.

Advertise your accomplishments. Humility has its place; but so does recognizing and sharing your accomplishments. Take credit for your successes, and do it in a big way. If you've made a significant difference inside your company, in your community or in the world, make sure others learn about you. Whether you are interviewing for a job, going for a raise, jockeying for a promotion, building your own business, or trying to get elected, a confident account of your accomplishments is not only necessary—it's expected. So don't live them down; live them up.

When the time is right, call a publicist; appear on panels; advertise your accomplishment on your web site; write a blog and post it on the wall of your Facebook page. This is your chance to let everyone see the real you; they will start to appreciate what a Fearless Fish can do. While you're at it, include your colleagues and the company you work for, or share how your work has benefited others. Sharing the spotlight takes the ego out of the mix.

When Barack Obama began his campaign for president, Chairman of DDB Worldwide Keith Reinhard said, "Barack Obama is three things you want in a brand: new, different, and attractive. That's as good as it gets." Obama built his brand and made himself relevant by embracing the Internet and creating a movement that amounted to an all-out call for change in the United States. He regularly updated his pages on social networking sites with photos, videos, and success stories, and made his own inclusive web site more dynamic than all the other candidates' sites by inviting his followers to create their own blogs and send policy recommendations. His campaign even provided a phone-bank widget to get call lists and scripts to tele-canvass from home.

The cutting-edge promotion of Obama's accomplishments actually invited others to participate in building a collective vision. Had John McCain (an older, less progressive candidate) done the same, it might have come off as a forced and strictly political tactic to gain votes. Obama was already different—a status that gave him an opening to campaign in a completely new way.

News flash: Building a recognizable and admired personal brand starts with being different and then doing something completely different. Patagonia founder and owner Yvon Chouinard is an extraordinary example of someone who has ignited a big change in the retail clothing business by turning his cause into a marketing strategy.

Yvon has built Patagonia—a supplier of top-quality outdoor goods—into a $230 million company without taking it public. He has, over time, maintained a generous attitude that has helped him nudge both colleagues and competitors in the direction of sustainability.

Patagonia was the first major retail company to switch to using organic cotton for its entire clothing line; the first to make fleece from recycled soda bottles; and the first to pledge one percent of its annual sales to grassroots environmental organizations. It has set a trend that has brands like The Gap, Levi's, Nike, and Timberland incorporating organic materials into their products while taking steps to minimize environment damage.

In Yvon's mind, the reason Patagonia exists is to put into action recommendations to avoid environmental collapse; to clean up America's act and to influence other companies and customers alike to do the right thing. Yvon decided to have Patagonia lead an examined life as a company and, as a result, revolutionized the industry. Patagonia has never made a single product using industrially grown cotton since it switched, and it's working fantastically. The move put the company on a completely different level from its competitors and it's influencing other companies to use organic cotton as well.

Yvon believes there is no such thing as complete sustainability, but it's possible to attain levels of it. It's a process, not a goal. All you can do is work toward it constantly.

One important lesson Yvon has learned is not to exceed your resources. "Try to live life on the edge, because that's when we get the most value; when we're really sticking our necks out and working at optimum efficiency.

"We're constantly being pulled toward complexity rather than simplicity. It has to start with each and every one of us to make change in our lives. It's up to each individual to lead an examined life."

Yvon's accomplishments have certainly been well advertised over the years. The outcome is that through Patagonia, he's been able to take a stand and maintain the company's vision—deriving a huge profit in spite of market forces and trends. He has *become* the trend, a trendsetter who is doing something definitive to create a better and sustainable world to live in.[2]

Two additional examples of people living examined lives—both of whom are focused on helping others, but in two very different arenas—follow. Both use their web sites and networks to illuminate the power and purpose of their causes. The first involves Safia K. Rizvi, senior director of influenza franchise marketing at GlaxoSmithKline, whom you learned about in Step 4.

I run a small nonprofit called eLIT (www.eLITonline.org). Its goal is to provide electronic literacy to underprivileged women in India and Pakistan. I started it in 2000, before I

---

[2]Based on "Don't Get Mad, Get Yvon" by Amanda Grsicom Little, Grist: Environmental News and Commentary, October 22, 2004.

went to business school. It gives me the chance to help people and provides me with the opportunity to gain skill sets and insight for myself. It's unrelated to the work I do in the pharmaceutical industry, and it opens my mind to thinking in different ways—integrating philanthropy with business, commercial market issues, and need—in order to find a way to generate revenue by these women for women.

GlaxoSmithKline has been very supportive of eLIT. The company donated used computers and has supported us through financial donations. Its acceptance and generosity has helped fuel the dual life I now lead. Ultimately, I want to be seen as equally competent in the nonprofit and for-profit worlds.

Then there's Will Halm—a gay, Asian-American father of three. Although few families of this composition exist, Will has built his professional life around these differences. He has been a gay community activist for a long time. That was the fuel that drove him to create the National Fertility Law Center and also to become chairman of the board for Growing Generations. He realized he needed to blend activism with his background as a corporate lawyer.

In the 1980s, Will and his partner wanted to have kids; so they began exploring having a family as a gay couple. Back then, the only adoption option for same gender couples was children that no one else wanted. The psychology community was not supportive of raising children without a mother. Very few gay couples were open about their relationships back then; and the high incidence of HIV/AIDS among same-sex couples raised a lot of questions and suspicions about the gay lifestyle.

I think that the gay community has evolved and grown up. First, it was about having fun, partying, and socializing; then community awareness and activism; then home and family. A lot of us started thinking about nesting.

What I have done [through the National Fertility Law Center] is to help gay men create families through surrogacy. In the past 10 years, the center has helped arrange the birth of more than 600 babies, almost all of whom have been placed with gay men—who are both single and in relationships.

Our company has helped create real breakthroughs for people who choose to go the surrogacy route. Our philosophy is "no judgments." So we support single people and those with partners, and help people from abroad create families. We even have the technology to safely use the sperm of HIV positive men. We've really pushed the envelope; doctors kept saying no, and we kept asking, "Why not?"

We feel a responsibility to the families we help create, and to other families headed by gay parents. There are a number of organizations that support these households—like Family Equality Council—and a lot of regional and statewide organizations like Rainbow Families out there to help gay families support each other. That mutual collaboration helps our company, because there are a lot of gay people out there who don't even know they can even have families. So I help illuminate those options through these organizations.

Safia and Will are both living proof that professional experience can be applied to personal causes that influence the world for the better. They each took it upon themselves to leverage their accomplishments to create groups around issues they were passionate about and made a difference. You can do the same—whether it's with coworkers, your company, outside organizations, or the entire planet.

Erica Huggins puts it this way: "I get calls from family, friends, and college students who want to get into the movie business. They all ask the same question: 'Should I go to film school?' My answer is: If you want to produce films, you have to have a point of view. To do that, you have to read books, travel, meet people. Follow your interests and passions and they will take you where you want to go. Get some experience before you go and make movies about other people's experiences."

The same can be said for just about any industry. Finding a balance between your work life and your personal life is an interesting challenge. One of the main points I'm making in this book is the fact that you can take what you've learned in both arenas and find a meaningful way to incorporate each into the other. Many people try to compartmentalize their lives. This is part of the reason people are struggling. They haven't learned to move fluidly between both worlds taking the best in each and finding an appropriate way to bring them together to create greater synergy. Who knows, you might find some very creative solutions to challenges you may be experiencing in either part of your life. Make no mistake: I'm not advocating treating your home life like a business or vice versa. Again, it's about taking the best in each, being resourceful, and creating something that uplifts not only your heart and spirits, but also the hearts and spirits of your coworkers. As Will Halm, chair of the board of Growing Generations, said: "Success follows commitment. I feel I'm so fortunate because my commitment led to professional and financial success while helping other people out there. It's very tangible."

Being an advocate—whether for yourself, for someone else, or for a greater cause—can be very rewarding. What it's all about is deepening the connection you have with yourself and your relationships. You may find, at least for a little while, that you need to do some advertising for yourself. That's okay. Advertising your accomplishments spurs your cause forward and inspires others to join you. So don't be shy about sharing your passion or your successes. Stay focused, be patient, persevere, trust yourself, and take a stand. You'll learn a lot, you'll expand and deepen your relationships, and the rewards will be immensely satisfying. All it takes is a willingness to put yourself out on the line!

Step 5 Exercises

Create a "Fix-It List."

List everything you are just tolerating right now in business:

1. _____
2. _____
3. _____
4. _____
5. _____
6. _____

List everything you are just tolerating right now in your personal life:

1. _____
2. _____
3. _____
4. _____
5. _____
6. _____

Out of all of these things, what would you prioritize at the top of your list to fix?

1. _____

2. _____

3. _____

What can you initiate in your organization that would advocate for the needs of others? Circle any that apply:

Green Initiative   Day Care for Working   Flextime
                        Parents

Diversity Training   Individual Coaching   Promoting
                                                 from Within

Team Building   Fair Wage Program   Management
                                                 Programs
Other

Is there a committee you could start?

How can you leverage your own personal power or that of your company to focus on a greater good in the world?

_____

_____

_____

Who can help you with this initiative?

_____

_____

_____

What steps do you need to take to make a difference?

_____

_____

_____

How will you market your accomplishments?

_____

_____

_____

How will raising your profile in this way at work help you in your career?

_____

_____

_____

Step

Evolve By Casting
a Wide Net

Fearless Fish Out of Water Know That Standing Still has Never Been a Long-Term Strategy for Moving Ahead

- Cultivate favorable variations.
- Add layers of uniqueness.
- Stay current.
- Give yourself time to evolve.

I remember waking up one morning in Santa Fe and feeling different about myself. I looked outside to see fresh snow covering our courtyard. Beyond our iron gates and stucco wall, the mountains looked strong and painterly. The snow was coming down softly, and the sun was shining through. It was like being inside a snow globe. I thought to myself, "This is it. This is the beauty and simplicity I've been seeking." The awareness and gratitude I had at that moment gave me the strength to see myself as someone who was evolving from a go, go city person to a quieter country person—from a consultant to a teacher, and from an art director to an artist.

It's said that Santa Fe either draws you in or spits you out. The evolution that was happening inside of me was necessary for me to be embraced by my new hometown. And it was happening naturally, like the seasons in the high desert.

The way to live deeply is to keep reinventing yourself.

Conformity is not distinguishing. The way to live deeply is to keep reinventing yourself, changing with the times and with the places you work and live while holding on to the essential you. It's also the fastest way to the top. Step 6 of being a Fearless Fish reveals the secrets of how to use your place outside the circle to always be relevant to your organization and industry. It's about staying true to the essence of who you are, and then recasting it to feel brand new.

Cultivate favorable variations. Evolution is essential— whether you were once the hot ticket whose star is now growing dim or you simply want to keep moving forward out of boredom; or perhaps you are feeling a need for change or see new opportunities on the horizon. When you're a fish out of water, the light is already shining on you. You're more visible and, therefore, more closely scrutinized. You can't be like one of those reality show contestants who go under the radar to stay in the game longer. You have to be the one who's playing to win. To do this, you must keep growing, stretching, and reinventing yourself.

Thom Beers, executive producer of such shows as *Monster Garage* and *Deadliest Catch*, knows this firsthand going from actor to corporate programming executive to independent TV producer—something that didn't exactly happen overnight or without some grit, sweat, and tenacity.

When I worked for Ted Turner, one of my first projects was for National Geographic in Brazil. I was producing a special about the Kayapo Tribe in the Amazon. When the project wrapped, I arrived back in Atlanta with my face completely tattooed. My fiancé almost fainted when she saw me. That story made me a legend at the company. That was nice, but how I even got there in the first place was memorable in a different way.

When I left New York for Atlanta to work for Ted, I'd been an actor, playwright, off-Broadway and commercial director. But before I got hired by Ted, my life was in the

> *toilet. I'd produced three TV commercials in one month: California pitted prunes, Preparation H®, and Scott® toilet tissues. Great!*
>
> *At that time, Ted was doing "save the world" stuff. So, I took a massive leap and reinvented myself. I sent Ted reviews, memos, letters—it took me four years to get a job with him. And when I did, I saw it as a huge opportunity to learn the business. I spent time with every division to get as big an education as I possibly could. I listened. You can have talent and ambition, but you also need to learn the tools. And I had to be fearless.*
>
> *The day came, though, when I needed to stretch myself, reinvent myself again in order to feed my soul. I left Ted to embrace the artists who were willing to do things differently from the Turner way of making a program—and it paid off. Corporations started knocking on my door for creative product.*

Someone else who understands this need—to constantly progress and grow—is one of my favorite artists, Mackenzie Thorpe. He calls his collection of new works *Evolution*. I came across a few of his striking bronze sculptures recently in New Orleans, a city that is in the throes of reinventing itself. The sculptures were intensely evocative, embodying the spirit of almost every artist: the passion to look further, to try different mediums to express oneself in new ways. "Stand still and die," is the belief that moves Mackenzie into his studio every morning, and it's what pulled him out of his working-class upbringing in Middlesbrough, England.

As the eldest of seven children, Mackenzie has evolved from a teenage shipyard worker to a celebrated artist exhibiting in museums and galleries across four continents. A true fish out of water, he struggled against dyslexia throughout his childhood.

He communicated with the world around him through painting and drawing, using whatever materials were at hand—including pencil stubs, eye shadow, and lipstick. Instead of allowing dyslexia to become his handicap, Mackenzie uses it to see things from a different perspective. It is a condition that has hindered so many, yet propelled him forward.

Becoming a professional artist wasn't an option in Mackenzie's hometown; however, he triumphed against the odds and is now among the most sought-after artists in the world. As he evolved, so has his ability to translate the entire range of human emotion: from the struggles and pride of working-class dockers to man overcoming great obstacles. "The paintings came before the sculptures, which I started creating about 10 years ago. My drawings and paintings were asking to walk off the paper and come alive," explains Mackenzie. From subject to medium, the evolution of the artist and his work is never complete.[1]

Another art form where evolution is essential is the entertainment industry—specifically for movie stars and child actors. In both film and television, personalities have come and gone. They were left behind in the dust of Hollywood's unquenchable thirst for whatever was newer, brighter, flashier, more daring, and more entertaining—all because they were unable to reinvent themselves. They saw only one avenue to success and paid the price.

Young actors like Susan Olsen from *The Brady Bunch*, Macaulay Culkin from *Home Alone*, and Oscar winner Tatum O'Neal from *Paper Moon* became so beloved that audiences were unwilling to accept the actors as having aged—so their careers diminished as they matured. It was very difficult for these younger actors to transition to more adult roles and at the same time keep their adoring—but fickle—fans happy. Unable to reinvent

[1]*New Zealand Press*, May 9, 2007; www.Mackenziethorpe.net

themselves, a number of child stars turned to drugs and alcohol—while others just disappeared from public view altogether.

A similar scenario is happening now in the corporate world. Workers who don't take the time to learn new computer skills as technology evolves are being passed over for promotions and in some cases, shown the door. It's like what occurred when computers and automation came into being. Many blue-collar industries switched from human-run production lines requiring many hands and bodies to machines that could do the same work at a fraction of the cost. Many people were let go as their companies refined and upgraded their processes. These people knew only one job; and the idea of making the move into the computer age seemed an insurmountable leap. Many floundered, were incapable of adjusting, and succumbed to depression or worse. They weren't able to find other meaningful work, because they'd boxed themselves in by thinking that they were good for only one thing.

The Fearless Fish out of water is interested in not just winning, but winning from the inside out.

Fearless Fish out of water embrace change. They're not just interested in winning, but winning from the inside out. Again, they're authentic to who they are, take stock of the environment they're in, and then figure out how they can refashion or reinvent themselves. They do so in a manner that complements their essential being and moves them into a new realm—inviting others to see them in a fresh way. Sounds complicated, yet it's one of the most natural states of development we can count on to keep us alive and thriving.

In his groundbreaking *Origin of the Species*, Charles Darwin wrote that, "Species . . . are still slowly changing by the preservation and accumulation of successive slight favorable variations."

Fish, for example, started out as jawless filter feeders with bony armor over a cartilaginous body. Over thousands of years, they developed functioning vertebrae, gills, fins, and jaws, physical features that gave them a feeding advantage.[2] The nature of career evolution isn't much different: You need to periodically evaluate what's working for you and what isn't; be willing to preserve your indelible qualities; and at the same time vary your look, your style, and your thinking in a way that's advantageous to your situation.

Many of the people I interviewed for this book have made and continue to make those "favorable variations"—evolving by expanding on what they know and love. Thom Beers went from a Broadway actor to a critically acclaimed television producer. Kim Deck evolved into a mediator after years of being a lawyer. Safia Rizvi added a business school degree to her Ph.D. so that she would understand both the science and business side of the pharmaceutical industry. To make this kind of shift, start by identifying your unique expertise and skills and discover ways to amplify them, so that you can tell the world your greatest story.

That's what Salma Hayek did. As a political science major who once aspired to be Mexico's president, Salma went from Mexican soap opera actress to international movie star. It wasn't easy to make that transition. When the 24-year-old actress arrived in Hollywood, she quickly learned that Latin actresses were mostly typecast as a mistress, maid, or local prostitute. Venting her frustrations on a late night talk show, she caught the eye of husband and wife film producing team Robert Rodriguez and Elizabeth Avellan who were captivated by her intelligence. They put her in two major movies and she began to break the stereotypes. Today, Salma is not only widely recognized as an Academy Award-nominated actress, but she also stars in, directs, and coproduces

[2]http://skywalker.cochise.edu/wellerr/students/armored-fish/armored-fish.htm

major motion pictures and television shows like *Ugly Betty*. She also stands out for her work fighting for immigrants' and abused women's rights. Every part of her fish-out-of-water story is a testament to the importance of career evolution.[3]

Influential companies often evolve their brands to stay relevant.

Influential companies often evolve their brands to stay relevant. Cadillac, for instance, is evolving to connect to a younger, hipper audience of drivers; Toyota has a significant presence in the expanding market for green solutions; Dove soap is now targeting women of all body types and ages by celebrating their range of beauty. These companies are just a few among dozens that understand that they must continue to appeal to consumers' changing tastes.

It's often adversity that spurs people and companies on to greatness.

Companies and people don't become irrelevant or obsolete because they suffer a loss, or experience an unexpected event or new challenge. They go into a decline because of what they do to themselves. That usually boils down to getting stuck in an old pattern, not staying true to what they do best, getting away from their mission, or biting off more than they can chew. The hard knocks that throw you off and cause you to falter don't have to be your downfall; in fact, it's often adversity that spurs people and companies on to greatness. It's also adversity that can help us discover what's really wonderful about being alive.

[3]www.imbd.com

When Borden Inc. started downsizing, my sister Wendy was offered a decent severance package for her years of loyal service. She had always been comfortable in a corporate role and as the company's presentation specialist, she had a steady paycheck, respect from coworkers, and the ear of the CEO. All of that was about to change.

Wendy put out a shingle and bravely started "Clarity Presentations," a boutique agency specializing in creating dynamic sales presentations. Eight years later, she has major clients like NetJets, Ohio Health, and The Limited. She also collaborates with Big Fish to create television network "upfront" presentations designed to attract ad dollars. Without that nudge out the door, she might have been in the corporate world forever, never getting the chance to dip her toe in entrepreneurial waters. Now Wendy has the flexibility to really be there for her family, and she has the pride that comes from working for oneself. None of that could have happened without a pink slip.

Sometimes you just have to walk in the desert thirsty and hot to appreciate the pleasure of soft rain. You can be a dinosaur and suffer career extinction because you are unable or unwilling to adapt to a changing marketplace; or you can disappear like the Neanderthals did because you were laid off and you can't see past the rejection. We can either follow the lead of those who died out wondering what happened and why it happened to us; or we can step up to the plate and play ball—on our own terms.

Stop asking, "Why do these things always happen to me?" and instead ask, "What can I be doing to move my career forward?" Dig deep to find your essence. Then do what you can to sharpen your unique talents and move on. As Helen Keller said, "To keep our faces toward change and behave like free spirits in the presence of fate is strength undefeatable."

News flash: To stay in the swim of things, Fearless Fish notice that the world is changing, and they evolve right along with it.

Fish out of water are all about thriving on change because change keeps things moving on an upward spiral.

As I stated in Step 5, change is not your enemy, it's your ally. Fish out of water are all about thriving on change because it's what makes life interesting. Change keeps things moving on an upward spiral. Becoming stale, complacent, stagnant—these options are unworthy for a Fearless Fish out of water. This might mean that you'll be presented with a change you feel you're not ready for— such as suddenly being made the head of your department, taking the reins on a new project, or being appointed to take your company in a whole new direction. Though this can be scary, it's happening for a reason and you actually have what it takes to face the challenge. Why? Because we are all served what we can handle and what we need to take on in order to fulfill our destiny. If something else were supposed to be happening, it would. Yes, you'll probably make some mistakes, but it's all about learning and growing and stretching. You can then take all the tools you're learning in this book and rise to the occasion. The fish out of water not only survives and thrives but also flies and soars!

Zeev Haskal, owner of Mega Group Investigations whom I mentioned in Step 3, offers his perspective on rising to the occasion and reinventing yourself.

During my stint with the Israeli Special Forces, I got very interested in photography and shot a lot of portraits, but that was only a hobby at the time. After the army, I moved to the United States with a camera and $500 in my pocket thinking I'd become a professional photographer.

Once I got to L.A., I realized I wasn't good enough to be a fashion photographer. In order to make money, I went to work for a security and investigations company. I worked full-time and took night classes at the Pasadena Arts Center College of Design. There I met my teacher's studio partner, an interesting character. He asked me to come with him to a photo shoot. He gave me a camera, one roll of film, and a model. The model said that they were the best photos anyone had ever taken of her. I showed my photos to the head of one of the largest modeling agencies in L.A. and she told me the photos were no good—they weren't art fashion photographs. My friend the photographer gave me another roll of film and helped me take fashion photographs that could be considered more artistic. I went back to modeling agency. The owner said she'd never seen lighting like that. That day, I had 30 girls from the agency call me for headshots.

I was now at a crossroads: Become a full-time fashion photographer or stick with the security and investigations company. Both paid close to nothing. At that time, I owed four months of rent, I had maxed out all my credit cards, I had no car, nothing. I was eating 99-cent tacos and telling my parents back in Israel that everything was great. Finally, I had to sell my camera. I opened the yellow pages and found an Israeli security company. They had no job for me, but I barreled my way in and convinced them to hire me. That night, I became Arnold Schwarzenegger's bodyguard.

I decided to build my own company, Mega Group Investigations. I made a pledge to myself to create a business based on integrity and professionalism. It took a lot of years, guts, and effort to get where I am today. I opened my business in 1992. Today our business comes 100 percent from referrals. We now work with some of the largest law firms in the country.

> *My experience with the Israeli Special Forces and Secret Services helped me to learn how to be tenacious. I'm like a cat. I'll always land on my feet.*

Zeev's love for photography brought him to the United States. Although he never became a fashion photographer, taking pictures is essential to his business. Ultimately, Zeev's ability to build on his unique skills and evolve them in the face of adversity made him a success.

So, what "favorable variations" can you make? Maybe it involves increasing your role in important projects; or moving into a new branch of your career. It may require going on a sabbatical, volunteering, trying new sports, teaching a class, or taking computer courses. It's time to think of what action you can take to reach your next peak and give you the strength to resist that doubting voice. When you stop being afraid of change, you can step into center stage—and a whole world of possibility will open up.

When you're on your path, things fall into place.

I believe we all have a reason for being here, and a legacy to leave. If we are open to it, we will be guided in the directions we need to go. When you're on your path, things fall into place. The right people come into your life to support your life's mission and the legacy you're destined to leave. But you have to help it become real by believing in it—even if you don't know exactly how it will come to be.

Zeev offers the following advice: "Keep your identity, but become an American. Learn English, learn the culture. Learn the people. Be about integrity, while you are trying to become someone. It went a long way for me. You build trust with someone, and they'll keep coming back and recommending you to others. Find ways to always get better."

Add layers of uniqueness. Long before there was paper, people wrote on animal hides. When they made mistakes or wanted a "do over," they did what they could to erase what they'd written; but the ghost of the old showed through the new writing. That's how it is in our lives, too. All of our experiences helped to shape our thinking and get us where we are today. Our job is to keep writing new stories, but never forget what we've learned so that we can keep on growing.

Over the past 16 years, my ad agency has reinvented itself several times. We started out in 1992 as a promotions firm handling sweepstakes and contests. When the business culture and advertising strategies evolved in the late 1990s, my interests evolved along with them. My company became a brand marketing firm, and by the new millennium, we had reinvented ourselves as a digital advertising agency. Today, we're known as a brand marketing firm and an interactive agency for "brands without borders." As we make this latest transition, I am becoming more visible by hosting panels at industry events, and by continuing to give motivational speeches and brand discovery workshops.

Notice that I stated "over the past 16 years" above. This is not something that happened overnight. That would be like saying someone became a star overnight, and forgetting that they've slaved and sweated for years before they were noticed. Adding layers of uniqueness is generally something that takes time, effort, patience, and tenacity. Everyone pays their dues, so to speak. It's called gaining life experience. And through that, you can determine what parts of your personality and character are in alignment with your work and which should be discarded because they represent old patterns and thinking that don't serve you.

Many examples of people who've done this abound—some did so through careful planning, and others by simply recognizing the opportunities before them. For some, it all happened rather quickly. Take actress and author Shirley MacLaine. When she was just 21, she was in the chorus of the Broadway show *Pajama Game*. One day, the show's lead, Carol Haney, broke her ankle. As her understudy, Shirley suddenly had to go on for Carol even though she didn't feel completely ready. Instead of calling it quits, she did as she had done years before when she sprained her own ankle: she tied the ribbons of her toe shoes very tight and went on with the show. Her star rose that night, and has shone brightly throughout her life.

For many of us, though, our choices are going to come less dramatically. Susan O'Meara, the American documentary filmmaker now living in Ireland, underwent a steadily progressive process of first becoming acclimated to a new country and culture. She then had to find her place and purpose for being there beyond the fact that Ireland is her ancestral home.

I call myself an ex-Patrick. Or maybe ex-Patricia is more accurate. Anyway, I'm a native of another country living in a new one from where my people come. I think I had more fantasy than fact in my heart and head when I first came here to live. I thought it would be easier, swifter, cozier—that I would slide into a fresh start. I had an innate, but often imagined, sense of belonging; here at my feet, on my doorstep, was the Ireland of my father's youth, the home he loved above all others.

Initially, I didn't take advantage of the clean slate that moving to Dublin offered me. I floundered, shuffled, went cross-eyed, and bumbled along outside of my U.S. comfort zone. But the gift that arose out of this initial fumbling was huge. Without those long-standing comforts, I eventually had to rally. I always thought of myself as an independent go-getter. In fact, I wasn't as self-reliant as I believed myself to be. Moving through the alienation of a new life in a new country where everything was new, I gradually became the self-sufficient, self-motivated individual I'd always dreamed of being. Nothing short of that was going to make me stronger—or strong enough.

Gradually I came out of my shell in Ireland. I joined a gym, got a therapist, took a wine course (where I met four fabulous female friends), became an even more voracious reader, joined a riding club, got out and about more, and traveled all over the country. I started documentary projects that brought me onto the farms of Ireland, and into the homes and kitchens and families of some of the country's most amazing food heroes— people who've never strayed from the land to make their living and make their mark. And I stayed put for awhile.

Whether you're a trout or salmon or tadpole or dolphin, swimming comes naturally even though you may cut the waves differently than your bigger or smaller counterparts. There's power in the school with other fish in the water, but there's greater schooling to be had by breaking away to ride your own current, by being a fish out of water. Just breathe. Deeply. Let the current guide you but be sure to make your own waves.

What qualities do you want to evolve to live bigger? In what new ways can you develop those qualities—all the while staying true to your essence? These are the layers. These are the rings of growth. The decision may be quick, the execution may take longer, but with focus and determination, the changes will come. So will the depth and expansion.

In a sense, we're similar to trees. If you cut a tree down, you'll see the rings of its life experience. Some of the rings are very narrow and others rather wide, with varying sizes in between. Each is a witness to that year's weather pattern. The large rings show us that water was plentiful that year, therefore, the tree grew a lot. Smaller rings mean less water, and even periods of drought. Sometimes, burned segments let us know there was fire. By studying the tree's rings, we get a cross section of its life journey. All the rings combined show the finished product, the outer expression. By cutting the tree down, we are privy to more of its inner life, its story.

Not that we're going to do that to humans—but within each of us lies a story, one comprising innumerable experiences that have helped us become the people we are today. And each of us is unique. Through this book, you're discovering just how unique and valuable you are—to yourself and to the world around you. As you take charge of your life, it's up to you to determine the layers you want to add to help you grow and support your being a fish out of water.

Stay current. A woman called me recently to discuss career opportunities. A seasoned producer of TV commercials and movie trailers, she had taken a two-year hiatus and at age 50, she wanted to get back in. I suggested she start by attending some television design conferences and exploring the new digital culture the television industry had adopted. "I'm way too old to be in that mix of people!" she protested. I realized right away why she was having trouble finding the work she wanted. With that attitude, she definitely is too old. She's *choosing* to be left out.

Evolution involves staying fresh and discarding old thinking.

Evolution involves staying fresh and discarding old thinking. Old thinking leads to exclusion. I bristle when I hear, "That's not how we did it at . . ." This statement shows me that the person who's speaking is not a creative thinker, not open to what's possible, and not forward thinking. It's also possible that such an individual has been in his current "box" so long he's forgotten *how* to be creative. Or he's become fearful of appearing too avant-garde or out of alignment with the company's vision and would rather play it safe. To put it simply, such a person is living in fear.

If you want to be involved and evolving, try welcoming change instead of fearing it—as so many people do. Fear of change can actually be seen as a judgment against yourself; a notion that you don't have what it takes, that you can't keep up. You're not fast enough, not bright enough, too old to learn new tricks. Is that so? Where did you ever get the idea that you can't cope with something? Like I said earlier, if you've been served a challenge, you are up for it. Yes, sometimes we get tired of having to take it all on. We feel piled upon and put upon. It can feel like being in school for the rest of your life. But don't despair and don't give in. Stay open to new opportunities until you take your last breath and your learning will not end until your life does.

Change is where the energy is, and that's where the Fearless Fish out of water needs to be.

Change is where the energy is, and that's where the Fearless Fish out of water needs to be. Sometimes, change happens and you respond; other times you have to initiate it to stay fresh. Be creative. Enroll in adult-education classes at your local university or community college, stretch yourself to learn and keep up with technological advancements and software programs. If you're beyond the 18- to 34-year-old demographic, you may want to join the world of social networking by building a Facebook or MySpace page, or becoming part of LinkedIn. You'll see what it's like to live in the digital world like so many younger people do. When you keep up with the ever-changing culture, the landscape of what's foreign to you shrinks—and so does the distance between you and others.

Enthusiasm is contagious and attractive. It is driven by passion and it feeds passion.

Enthusiasm is another essential for staying current with the times. Enthusiasm is contagious and attractive. It is driven by passion and it feeds passion. It keeps you from getting old and tired while you grow and mature. It's what you fall back on when you're a fish out of water—it can be your guiding light. H Lewis serves as a good example here again. He's led a team of successful salespeople by being what his boss refers to as "the poster child for speaking up and living to survive it." H raises his hand at company-wide open forums and at meetings for vice presidents and higher-ups in a culture that is Southern—in other words, polite and nonconfrontational. "My curiosity and questioning inspires others to be open and honest," he says. H attributes much of his ability to change the way things are done at The Weather Channel to his being different. People can't ignore him; he stands out partly because of his visible passion for his work. And because of that passion, people listen and try out his ideas.

When I get a new product to work on, I look for its best qualities and its potential, and then I fall in love with it. My demeanor, my writing, and my ideas all express my enthusiasm about the product. That energizes my client and their sales team. So often, people closest to a product can only see its flaws. They're working so hard to overcome them that they can't envision the possibilities and potential anymore. My love for their product helps them take it to the next level. And that's money in the bank.

How is your enthusiasm expressed at work? What do you do that feeds your fire? Fish out of water need that extra boost to be exceptional, to be authentically dynamic. If you aren't driven by passion for what you do, find it and bring it center stage.

You might be thinking, "Fine, but what if I *really* don't like this project that I'm being offered?" You have several options, some of which I've covered in earlier steps. The option I want to throw out to you here is this: an attitude shift. If you really don't like what's before you, it may be that you just aren't hip to change; it's not comfortable for you. I'm suggesting that you try to see past what you dislike and find something that's agreeable to you. It may be very subtle, or it may be grand, but it's up to you.

You have to evolve your style to stay current.

Madonna is proof that staying power can come from re-inventing yourself without ever compromising your core. The mother of reinvention, she's made evolution her survival strategy for more than two decades. She's continuously building her image around her interests and taking her adoring public along with her. At 50, she's on tour with another dazzlingly successful album. We've seen her morph from material girl to sex goddess, from 1970s disco queen to hip mother and spiritual yogi. She's always in top physical shape, always sexy, always bold; she always has a plan and a direction; and she plays her role to the hilt. There's a lot to learn from Madonna.

Stay alert to the times and make those subtle shifts that keep your energy fresh and present.

News flash: You're a fish out of water and you're different; here's your chance to make the most of it. Staying current doesn't mean you need to run out and get the newest gadget, hairstyle, fashions, or anything else. It may simply require reading up on the latest developments that are a part of your field; scanning television programs just to get an idea of what people are interested in; doing some research on the Internet to see what the most popular sites are and then checking them out; visiting YouTube to see what people are watching; getting together with friends or colleagues to find out where their heads are at about any given subject.

The possibilities are endless. How you go about evolving can expand your circle of friends, deepen your work relationships, and—most important—positively impact how you feel about yourself. You are a work in progress, a diamond in the rough—born to be lustrous and multifaceted. Staying current is only going to add to your sparkle!

Give yourself time to evolve. When I first came to understand that being different is a good thing, I thought I'd feel great all the time. What a relief after all those years of worrying that I didn't fit in! But my self-esteem issues were still there in the morning.

It's not about flipping a switch. As much as we may want to, we don't change overnight. Change is a continual process. Even Michelangelo said, "I am still learning." Oprah admits she's not perfect. Think of people you admire and consider their career paths. Did they arrive overnight? Did their path have spreading branches? Mine certainly did.

> *My career evolution has taken me into writing and public speaking, something that's happened over a period of several years. The shift began when one of my mentors suggested I share my ideas about personal branding with a wider audience. I liked the idea.*

To prepare, I took an extension course at UCLA on the power of persuasive speaking—and loved it. A few months later, I gave a keynote speech on personal branding to an audience of more than 100 women. Their enthusiasm confirmed for me that this was an important path. The next year, I wrote a book on personal branding, and I went on to give talks on the subject around the country. A few years later, I was ready to assess my life again.

To do this, I sat with my past to arrive at what would be my future. I had left the broken home of my childhood and now had a happy marriage; I had survived a neglectful mother to become an attentive and nurturing mother to my daughter; I had traded my youthful unease in business for confidence, purpose, and professional success. Still, I felt a bit lost. I was ready to live more fully.

I needed to realign with my core values—my health, my family, and what I love to do best. I identified what that is and decided how to bring it center stage in my life. Now I live in Santa Fe, and I'm starting to explore ways to become more deeply conscious while devoting myself to writing, public speaking, mentoring, teaching, and working with companies that want to make a difference in the world. This is the evolution that works for me.

Rome wasn't built in a day, as the saying goes. Your personal evolution will take time, too. It will be different for each person. You may be right on the cusp and primed for change. Or you may want to let all this information percolate, then make your move. It's up to you—it's your timetable.

This is life's journey. Be patient and compassionate with yourself. Embarking on anything new can be uncomfortable, even when you're finally recognizing who you are and are following your true calling. When you start walking in your own shoes, it can take some time for them to mold to the perfect shape that's right for you.

This step has been all about evolving by casting a wider net. As a fish out of water, casting a wider net has three interesting ramifications. One is that you're going to find pearls of wisdom to enhance the knowledge you already possess. Second, you're going to attract work that resonates with you and others like you who will be in step with you on your journey. And third, as you evolve, so will those around you. It's a win-win situation.

A word of warning—be mindful of your expectations. What I stated in the previous paragraph is true; but you also need to be circumspect in the process. People will be people, and each will have individual responses that need to be taken into consideration. Not everyone is going to understand you. They may *eventually* get what you're about, or they may decide not to walk along beside you. That's okay. Fish out of water need to be fluid. Yes, you can have passion—as we discussed in Step 1—but manage your expectations in the process.

It is very disheartening to invest in anything with big expectations only to have them dashed when they aren't realized as you'd hoped. It's hard to be creative and engaged when your expectations haven't been met. Therefore, the best approach is to be thoughtful and detached so that you are able to easily roll with the punches. The more we're invested in specific outcomes, the greater our disappointment will be if they don't work out as planned.

So the big lesson here is to cast wide your net and see what you reel in. If you remain neutral yet centered, you may find yourself surprised by what you catch, and the more easily you'll see the gift inherent in what you've caught. This is the crux of your evolutionary process: Everything, if perceived as a gift, is something you can use to your personal benefit.

Evolution of the species is one thing; evolution of the individual is everything. Evolution keeps you relevant, interesting, and ultimately more desirable. Just remember, evolution takes time, so be kind to yourself and be patient knowing that your journey is one of discovery, including cultivating favorable variations, adding layers of uniqueness, and staying current.

Step 6 Exercises

Evolution is essential to survival in business and in life.

How relevant are you? (Check those that apply.)

___ **Passion:** Are you feeling passionate about your work? Do your current projects and the people you work with excite you and share your values?

___ **Style:** Do you look the part you are playing or want to play? Does your exterior reflect your interior and your creative energy? Do you look contemporary?

___ **Support:** Do you have a cast of mentors, coaches, friends, and/or family there to support you? Have you checked in with them this week?

___ **Honesty:** Can you deliver on what you're promising? (Beware of overhyped communications.)

___ **Integrity:** Are you walking your path with integrity, or just playing politics?

___ **Fresh:** Have you tried something new this week? Taken a risk? Done it differently from the way it's been done before?

___ **Quality:** Does what you're doing meet the high standards of quality that you and your company and clients expect and deserve?

___ **Demand:** Are you in demand? Do people seek you out for your counsel and expertise?

___ **Interactive:** Have you engaged someone and inspired her or him to action?

___ **Energy:** Are you showing your enthusiasm for your product and/or projects? How's your energy level at work?

___ **Focused:** Have you prioritized effectively? Did this week's accomplishments speak to your company's bottom line and business objectives?

___ **Nurturing:** Did you do something this week that made you feel good about yourself? Did you show a coworker how much he or she means to you?

___ **Gratitude:** Did you experience joy this week and say thanks for that gift?

___ **Expectations:** Have you been realistic about meeting objectives and deadlines? Are you setting the bar too high, only to disappoint yourself and others?

___ **Professional:** Are you creating win-win partnerships? Being courteous and respectful to yourself and others?

What favorable variations can you make to help you evolve to become more relevant and give you the strength needed to resist your doubting, inner voice?

___ Move into a new area of your business
___ Volunteer

___ Go on a sabbatical   ___ Try a new sport

___ Teach a class   ___ Take a class that
                                    interests you

Other: _____

_____

_____

What old ideas can you let go of so that you can experience a renewed way to approach work?

_____

_____

_____

_____

What qualities do you want to evolve to live bigger and stay current?

_____

_____

_____

_____

In what new ways can you develop those qualities, all the while staying true to your essence?

_____

_____

_____

_____

How is your enthusiasm expressed at work? What can you do to feed your fire?

_____

_____

_____

_____

Write a mantra, a sentence, or find a quote that inspires you to evolve. Then, put it somewhere visible (your screen saver, in a picture frame, or on your mirror).

_____

_____

_____

_____

_____

Step

Reel in Your Unique Power

**Fearless Fish Out of Water Trust Their
Instincts and Have the Courage and
Belief in Themselves to Take Action**

- Believe in yourself.
- Have courage.
- Take action.
- Trust your instincts.
- Live big, go deep.

I was three years old when my mother put my sister and me in our brand-new, mint green Rambler station wagon. As she walked back into our house, we waited for her to tell my father good-bye for the last time. I was crying because I was sure it was my fault we were leaving. The day before, my father had scolded me for drawing on the walls with crayons. I held my baby sister and told her I was sorry. Wendy's little pigtails brushed my tears as she looked up at me with her big brown eyes, "Is Daddy coming on the trip?" she asked. "I don't think so," I answered. And then we both cried together.

My mother stumbled out of the house tucking a bobby pin into her red beehive hairdo, dressed in sleek, stretch black pants and a V-neck black sweater. She slid next to us on the bench seat, lit a Pall Mall, and put the car in reverse. As she turned the wheel, she looked at the two of us and said, "Girls, dry your eyes, we're going on an adventure!"

When my mother lost custody of my sister and me two years later, I felt unworthy and ashamed. It has taken me most of my life to realize that the divorce and my mother's inability to raise us or see us again was not my fault. To unshackle this weight, I cultivated an unrelenting curiosity about my own psychology. I went on the great adventure my mother had promised—only by myself. I was smudged by a shaman, attended a happiness workshop, banged a pillow with a baseball bat, wrote letters to my mother that were never sent, cast stones of shame into the Pacific Ocean, studied with a metaphysical coach, and sat at the feet of gurus—all in an effort to know who I am, the real me, and to love that person.

So much of what happened at work in my 20s and 30s (for better or for worse) had to do with putting my bosses and clients in parental roles. I dutifully worked to please them and sought their approval to become perfect in their eyes so that I could never be abandoned again (read: no boundaries). If it wasn't for my father who said, "I love you" every day, coupled with my innately hopeful spirit and quest toward self-discovery, I don't know if I could ever have practiced the ABCs for fish out of water—action, belief, and courage.

Feeling like a fish out of water comes largely from comparing ourselves to others. Add criticism from bosses and coworkers and the ultimate insult of being excluded, and it's hard *not* to perceive yourself as different, disconnected, and discounted. To deal with situations like this in the past, I would put on different masks: the follower, the caretaker, the party girl, the performer. I've had to peel off these self-defensive layers over the years to see myself as I am. There are times when I still catch myself putting on a mask. During our move to Santa Fe, one of our moving trucks was stolen from in front of our house in Los Angeles. It contained valuable, irreplaceable artwork created by my husband's deceased mother, representing every phase of her life's work. She was the only real mother I ever had. We both were devastated. We decided that we would not store our remaining possessions in the warehouse owned by the movers but rather move them to another facility.

The day of the transfer, the owner of the negligent moving company was angry and abusive toward me and I let him get to me. Basically, I did a "poor me" routine that just added fuel to his fire.

The next day, I set my intention on being the real me and took back my power. I told him that today would not be like yesterday. He was not to speak to us in any way unless it was professionally. He knew I meant business, and because of that he then did his job. I turned a toxic situation into a healthy one by taking off the mask that no longer worked for me—and probably never did.

Many of us have had something happen that rocked our world and made us question our personal value and the value of others in our lives. That's the common denominator for all fish out of water. Some of us handle this by becoming impatient or critical of ourselves and others. Some of us try to become the caretaker or control everything and everyone around us, so that the attention is not on us. And some of us even withdraw into ourselves deciding that because we don't fit in, we are in the wrong and therefore worthless and not needed. The fearless among us, though, go in another direction altogether: We celebrate our triumphs, find inner strength from these victories, and lead with greatness.

When I asked Thom Beers of Original Productions how he became a success, he said, "I had to be fearless. You have to have an innate hunger in your stomach for something. You have to be relevant. My junior and senior year of high school, my family was on welfare—we ate spam and stole shoes. When you come from nothing, you can roll over and concede defeat or work yourself through college and go after it. Tenacity is key. I never disappointed anyone. No matter the job, I didn't fail. I did, however, get fired from one of my jobs. It was the worst thing that could happen to me, but I was okay with that. I accepted being fired for taking a risk. 'Don't worry about the mule being dead. You just keep loading the wagon,' Joel Westbook, my former boss at Turner Broadcasting, told me."

Action
Belief
Courage

Thom's fears and my fears are no bigger or smaller than yours. For me, I just consciously transcend them through (A) purposeful *action*, (B) powerful and positive *belief* about my abilities, and (C) the *courage* that comes from knowing that if I've succeeded before, I can do it again.

When I give a keynote speech or I'm pitching new business for my agency, I am putting myself in the position of being judged. It's a truly scary yet exhilarating experience. To get to the point of having the confidence to stand up in front of strangers, to talk about myself and my work, I had to practice the ABCs. Action involved studying the craft of professional speaking, writing my presentation, and practicing every day. My belief came from telling myself that I could captivate an audience. The courage came when I walked onto the stage and realized that we are all really one because we're all looking for and wanting the same basic things in life.

It took years of action, belief, and courage to get to where I am today. Belief inspired my courage, having courage led me to action, my actions strengthened my belief, and my belief fed my courage—they all work together. In the past, I would be swayed by others' opinions because I was so eager to please. Today, I trust my instincts and I rely on them. I trust that when I take the leap, the action I've taken is the right one.

So, how do you find the belief in yourself to get out of bed each day and go on when life has thrown you one too many curveballs? How can you tap into the courage it takes to live big when you can't get on equal footing? What actions can you take when it feels like the world is placing obstacle after obstacle before you?

As a filmmaker, Susan O'Meara, whom you met in Step 3, is interested in other people's journeys, but she had to do some traveling herself to finally come to the realization of where she felt she belonged in this world—a place that fed her soul—and it took action, belief, and courage to get there.

From Kenya to Kazakhstan, I went both to lose and find myself as only travel can do. I sampled rough and ready roads alike, many brand new, some exotic, others nostalgic. I drank mare's milk in the Tien-Shan Mountains (Celestial Mountains) of Central Asia, an intoxicant that tastes of horse sweat. I napped on the leather floor of a hut in a Maasai manyatta *(village) in Tanzania. I visited a Kazakh orphanage and ate barbecued lamb—I think—from a pictures-only menu. I followed a warrior along the Ewaso Ng'iro River in Samburu National Reserve in Kenya, nearly colliding with a rascally herd of bachelor elephants.*

Then, one afternoon, I climbed over the Conor Pass in Dingle, County Kerry—and there before me was a flame and lavender sunset that rivaled any I'd seen in East Africa. I wanted to stay in Ireland.

I then began a process of integrating myself into my new home of choice—Ireland. I didn't settle easily or quickly into my little red brick cottage in Dublin—or my neighborhood or community. I kept to myself, understanding that getting to know the Irish can be tricky. Charming, inquisitive, seemingly open, they've learned through centuries of occupation and oppression and conflict to be slow to reveal, to hold back, to keep you at arm's length when you think you're already well into the kitchen!

For example, if you ask an Irish person how he's doing, he might reply, "Poorly, thank God." He wouldn't want you to think he's putting on airs or that he's doing so well he might have something you want.

I've made friends, but slowly, the slowest I've ever moved socially in my entire life. When my parents passed on, I wrote both their eulogies. I wrote my heart out, and those two pieces, those memories on paper, are the things I'm most proud of ever having written. While this didn't strengthen any sense of belonging to my new home, my father's homeland, it did set me on a path of living my life out in passion.

The final step in my book is all about finding the inner strength to go on no matter what happened to you in your past or what's being put in front of you in the present. It's all about solidifying the process of getting to the top of your game as the distinctly unique individual you are: Believe in yourself, have courage, take action, trust your instincts, live big and go deep.

Believe in yourself. Jack Canfield and Mark Victor Hansen, creators of the *Chicken Soup for the Soul* series, were turned down by more than 50 agents before they found one who believed in the project as much as they did. The manuscript was then rejected by more than 200 publishers before one finally took a chance on it. The series, which today boasts 105 titles, has sold over 100 million copies in more than 40 languages. They believed, they never gave up, and look what happened.

Walt Disney went to 100 banks trying to secure a loan for a project he had in mind called Disneyland. All the banks turned him down. Then, the 101st bank said, "Yes." And the rest is history. Walt found someone who believed in him and his project. The other 100 banks are kicking themselves for not having had the courage to take a leap of faith with Walt. And the good thing, for the rest of the world, is that Walt continued going from bank to bank until he found the right one. He was steadfast in his dream and in his belief in himself.

What you believe about yourself can lead the way. It's up to you.

News flash: What you believe about yourself can lead the way. It's up to you. As a fish out of water, you're alone out there without others like you around to confirm that you're on the right path or doing your best work. You can strengthen your belief in yourself in a number of ways. For starters, create a solid support team as we discussed in several previous steps. This includes finding a mentor, joining a professional organization, or nurturing friendships with people who understand you.

Being your own cheerleader is also key. Why not root for your own team? First, acknowledge your own accomplishments—take notice of what you've achieved before you rush on to whatever's next. It pays to take time to reflect on what's positive in your life—after all, what you give your attention to increases. Alison Hays, a graphic designer, has a creative way of acknowledging her accomplishments. Alison works from home and doesn't have others around her to pat her on the back, so she likes a physical representation of these "pearls" in her life. She hangs a string of faux freshwater pearls on the wall by her desk and she adds a pearl to it every time she accomplishes something important to her. Seeing the necklace grow longer energizes her.

Erica Huggins of Imagine Entertainment has an interesting spin on believing in yourself.

> *People are always surprised when they Google me on the Internet. They see what I've done, and that I'm not some cranky old person. The younger generation is shocked that I have two children and that I look hip. There's another Erica Huggins who was with the Black Panthers in the 1960s. Several times, people have expected a black woman to walk into the room—and that's actually landed me several film projects, all based on mistaken identity.*
>
> *In spite of that, I've maintained my true identity, which can be especially difficult in L.A. In the film business, you make a choice between being a Brian Grazer—a huge producer who runs the show—or a person who works for him. When I had children, I decided on the latter. I knew who I was—I have a point of view, I have a gut, and I know how to say "no" and stand by my decisions. I will tell people the truth in a city where most people don't. I was told over the years that it was okay to slip and slide but working without integrity can come back to bite you. So, I've learned to be honest and be myself.*

Acknowledge the people who support you.

The second key is to acknowledge the people who support you—they not only get you, but they are accomplished in their own right. What they're about meshes with who you are and vice versa. You are, indeed, a team!

Building belief in yourself means shedding negative beliefs.

Now, here is one of the most important keys for believing in yourself: Building belief in you also means shedding negative beliefs. ("I'm not good at sales," "I'm disorganized.") The beliefs you have about yourself are integral to your being able to feel and be successful—according to your own rules. So here's something you can do that will definitely be of help. Make a list of your beliefs. Making a list of what you believe about yourself can be eye opening. First, list all the positive beliefs you have about yourself. Then, create a list of all the negative beliefs you have about yourself. Once you've finished these lists, ask yourself which of these beliefs are your own and which may be others' beliefs about you. It's possible that what you believe and what others believe about you isn't even close to the truth. The question to ask yourself at this point is: Why am I supporting these beliefs about myself that aren't even true?

You must take charge of you.

It's decision-making time. Either you're going to let these beliefs that are not true about you run your life, or you're going to let them go and take charge. This is very important. You, as a fish out of water, will never be the incredible and fully accomplished person you can be unless you completely take charge of your life. No one really likes having others tell them how to think, be, feel, dress, talk, and act.

If you are living your life according to others' beliefs about you, then it's time to make a major change. You can do it! It may feel a little uncomfortable at first, and your relationships with some people may change somewhat, but it's about you being the authentic you. And if you're operating according to some false beliefs about yourself that you have bought into, then this process will be that much easier—because you have only yourself to work with.

News flash: Be sure you're aware of your feelings throughout this process. As you review the beliefs you've listed, the ones that aren't truly yours may evoke feelings of powerlessness; you're stuck with them; they're calling the shots. Wrong!

I categorize these reactions as simply "phantom feelings"— beliefs that *appear* to have power over you. The reality is that they actually don't have any power over you, you're letting them do so. You alone are in charge of your feelings. You decide how you're going to feel about and respond to everything. For instance, no one makes you mad or sad or happy or silly. If you're letting others push your buttons, then you've chosen to give them your power. This does not work for fish out of water. You make the choice.

The third part of this process is to list your biggest accomplishments, whatever you are most proud of having done. Beneath each item on this list, write what belief or beliefs about yourself have helped you get where you are. It's a revealing process that can quickly lead to a turnaround in how you see yourself, how you live, what you project, and what innate potential you possess.

Now you've got a strong and clear understanding of the beliefs you live by, the ones that truly support you. You may be feeling a little unsure about how you're going to consistently live by the new choices you've made, so what comes next is the third pillar of the ABCs: courage.

Have courage. Remember these famous words: "I haven't any courage at all. I even scare myself!" The Wizard of Oz knew these words weren't true. He said to the Lion, "As for you, my fine friend, you are a victim of disorganized thinking. You are under the unfortunate delusion that simply because you run away from danger, you have no courage! You are confusing courage with wisdom." He then pinned a medal of courage, the Triple Cross, on the Lion's chest.

It takes courage to follow your heart and go after what you want.

We all deserve a medal pinned on our chests. We're courageous every time we step out the door and say "yes" to living our truth, being boldly different from the rest of the world. It takes courage to follow your heart and go after what you want. Thom Beers could have stayed an actor instead of challenging himself to become an independent producer. Kim Deck could have remained an attorney instead of moving into mediation. I could have stayed in the South where I had friends and connections, instead of moving myself and my fledgling business across the country. It was culture shock coming to Los Angeles, but I found the courage deep inside me to build a life there by believing that I could make it. That kind of courage spurred my husband, Steven, to become successful as my partner at Big Fish.

Robin invited me to join her company in 1999 to start the online division. Only, I didn't know anything about the Internet. I had never worked in marketing or advertising, and I didn't have a clue about the cable television business. Plus, I had never worked at a small company, only major movie studios and talent agencies. I basically put myself in a situation where I was a complete fish out of water.

My first meeting was with five executives on an existing project. We had to design the Fox Family Channel affiliate web site. Add to the list of things I knew nothing about: designing or building web sites. Despite this, I nodded at what I felt were the appropriate times. I had no idea what anyone was talking about.

Robin believed in me. That's why I was at the table. I had success as an executive and producer in the movie business and Robin thought she could harness my intelligence, people skills, and sales ability to launch Big Fish into the world of online marketing and advertising. So, we created a name for this new Internet division and called it Fishnet. And immediately after announcing the new division publicly, many of our clients gave us assignments because they assumed I had experience in the Internet space and that, coupled with Robin's cable marketing expertise, made a perfect match in their minds.

So I figured the only way I would actually learn how to do my job well was to hire vendors and creative partners who knew the Internet and learn from them. This was the action I took.

My naiveté became my advantage. Because I didn't know how things worked, I tended to try ideas that were novel and ask for higher fees from clients. I didn't know any better and it seemed to work out. I became a sponge for any knowledge or insight, and put it to use every day, inventing creative ways to engage audiences online and get them to watch the TV shows we were promoting. In this way, I established a new division that become profitable from the day we opened the doors.

Necessity is the mother of invention. I had left the movie business because I didn't feel there was a future for me there. The Internet thing was happening and I figured that there must be some similarities, and there were. I took my job seriously and worked hard to put our company on the cutting edge of online marketing. I attended loads of industry trade conferences with Robin, which became a big part of my education and networking. My belief in myself and the courage that I mustered came from doing all of this, but mostly it came from partnering with my wife. She made sure there was a net if I fell.

It all comes down to remembering how courageous you already are.

It's all about meeting the challenges you face with courage—whether it's taking on a new position, going away to college, learning a new language, skiing for the first time, or opening your heart to a perfect stranger in the hope that he or she might become your life partner. Just think about everything you've done in your life that was brave and you'll see yourself that way.

Jason Heller, former managing director of Horizon Interactive and founder and CEO of DivePhotoGuide.com, stated it very well.

Being true to myself is my basic principle of life. Knowing what makes me truly happy fosters passion. My business acumen and experience in the marketing world helps the rubber meet the road, and drives me to merge my passion with the realities of creating a market for myself. The result has been a multipronged business that includes a niche media company as well as a photography production business (JasonHeller.com).

I've always had the courage to go for my dreams. I'm willing to make the sacrifice on the way up, and once

*engaged in the process, will never turn back. I will suc-
ceed, period.*

*There are two sides to me (creative and business)
and I don't let society define me. I work solely based on my
passions and motivations in life. Bottom line, I'm committed to clients who want to be successful. I can then
connect with their winning attitude and passion for the
Internet. But, first they have to be committed to themselves. I don't want to work with people who are not
innovative, who don't want to be risk takers.*

*I'm passionate about what I do. I love what I do. I don't
have a formal education. But, I'm very educated on my
industry: the intense dynamics, the incredible growth,
what it means to society. Excellence is a differentiating
virtue.*

Take action. When no one gets you, taking action takes a lot
of resolve. There's opportunity in any challenge. I have a client
who moved around a lot as a kid. His father's job took the family to
far-flung places, and he had to adapt. Now he's comfortable being
an Englishman in New York and loves the adventure. He's
teaching his kids how to live in a world that requires flexible,
out-of-the-box thinking and they're thriving.

Letting go of expectations for a particular outcome helps.

Taking action has so much to do with being open to the
unknown, readying yourself for what will be and realizing that if it
doesn't work out, you just learned what not to do. Letting go of
expectations for a particular outcome helps. You can visualize a
positive conclusion and then tell yourself that no matter what

happens, you are grateful for the opportunity. If you do everything to prepare, then you're golden. You can be satisfied knowing that you gave it your best shot. When things don't go their way, Fearless Fish figure out what went wrong, regroup, and take action again.

Susan O'Meara has this to say about believing in yourself and learning along the way.

> *Don't look back. It's not the direction you're going, it's not the direction the Earth, time, the elements, stars move in. Look forward. Embrace mistakes as the learning tools that they truly are. Martha Beck recently said that the most successful people are those who have failed the most. There's no good, bad, or ugly—there's just what happens and what doesn't.*

Kim Deck, a top employment mediator takes action by constantly marketing herself to law firms needing her services to help resolve disputes out of court.

> *I believe in staying in front of people. I go to lots of conferences and speaking events. I write articles to get in legal trades. I also send postcards and letters to current and prospective clients. I call the people I know and build strong relationships. My goal is to make five contacts each day. I know that not all of those contacts will result in business, but I have put myself out there to keep the cases coming my way.*

It's important when you're taking action to create a context for what you're trying to sell. A while back, I had a client who just couldn't understand or appreciate how great his online campaign was performing because his company had never advertised on the

Internet. In a results meeting, we were throwing numbers at him for click through and interaction rates (terms that mean the number of times viewers click to a site from an online ad and how long they spend interacting with that ad). All the while, we were telling him how proud and excited he should be. He just shook his head and said, "This just seems so low," and, in his mind, it did—because he had no benchmarks by which to measure performance. The next meeting, I showed him how his competition was doing spending triple his ad budget online—their poor performance against his stellar results. A lightbulb went on, instantly creating an appreciation for what we were doing.

It's all about preparation and performance.

News flash: We can get so wrapped up in our own ideas no one can relate to us. As a fish out of water, it's your job to find a common language and that comes from understanding what's important to the person you're trying to influence. It's all about preparation and performance. The *action* it takes to do things right lives inside of you. It's stepping outside your fear to take that action that makes all the difference.

Doing nothing can be a good strategy, especially when you don't know what to do.

As long as we are on the subject of taking action, it's important to note that sometimes *inaction* can be the right course to take. That's right. Doing nothing can be a good strategy, especially when you don't know what to do. If you sit quietly, the answer can come to you. On the other hand, stopping yourself from doing the one thing that could make you happy is self-sabotaging. Not doing what needs to be done usually comes from overthinking a situation. When you analyze things too much, you can become paralyzed. That's why the next subject is an integral component of the ABCs.

Trust your instincts. "I have a good gut," says Nathalie Lubensky. "I go by my intuition. It's the Haitian voodoo piece of me, the Holy Spirit, God answering my prayers and telling me what to do." Nathalie prides herself on this, knowing it's how she needs to navigate in her business environment. I do the same thing: I listen to my gut for big and small answers all the time. I moved to L.A. because I wanted to focus on television, and L.A. was home to many television networks and the entire entertainment industry. I had recently left Turner Broadcasting to go out on my own, and the legendary Brandon Tartikoff (former president of NBC and chairman of Paramount Pictures) said to me, "You should be in Los Angeles." So, I moved six weeks later. It was a radical move—one that would turn my life upside down—but I had a *gut feeling* he was right.

News flash: Trusting your instincts is especially important for the fish out of water. There's no script to follow because you're writing your own story, something no one else can do for you. You have to pay attention to the clues that can help guide you. Look for the signs, and, when they come and they feel right, jump in, even if your knees are knocking. After you jump, take a deep breath, and keep trusting your instincts. You've made the leap, you know it was right, you'll make whatever adjustments are needed as the situation evolves.

Imagine how different the world would be if we all held back and didn't trust our intuition, our gut feelings. Think what we'd be missing: Rudolf Nureyev, Mikhail Baryshnikov, and Martina Navratilova would never have left Russia. Pablo Picasso would have remained just another painter. Madame Curie would have stayed in the shadows of her husband. Martin Luther King, Jr. would most likely be just another preacher. Helen Keller would never have discovered the world as we know it and shared it from her unique perspective. The list goes on and on. Essentially, we'd still be back in the Stone Age, afraid to test ourselves, afraid to take a risk.

I believe we create our own destiny through the choices we make, but, at the same time, there is a greater power in the universe that offers guidance if we are open to hearing it. I practice hearing it every morning by sitting in a short meditation, palms open, and saying, "I'm ready for what's next. I want to do what's needed of me. I have talent, and I'm open to using it in the best possible way." It's a prayer, an intention, a specific request to the universe to show me signs, give me guidance I can follow as I pursue my path. That openness has brought me to a lot of new places.

Openness to trusting instincts has brought a lot of other people places, too. The trick is listening, believing, and being willing to go for it when your intuition speaks loud and clear. Steve Jobs knows this. He told a Stanford graduating class that "You have to trust in something—your gut, destiny."

I've said it before and it's worth repeating. Every mistake I've ever made happened when I didn't listen to my gut. Balancing the messages from your mind (intellect), your heart (emotions), and your soul (inner knowledge) is the key. Just thinking your way through won't work. You have to combine rational thought with emotional knowledge and the wisdom of your inner voice.

When I take my dog for a hike, I'm all alone with my higher power and all the beauty around me; that's when the messages come. Make a pledge to yourself that you'll find a time of day when you can just listen, then follow the signs that lead you in the right direction. If you don't think you can find a time, if your schedule is too busy, think back to a time when you trusted your intuition, when you saw the signs and you acted accordingly. What were those signs? What action did you take? How did it go? Was there a time you didn't listen to yourself? How did *that* go? What did you learn from that experience? I think you'll find that if you do this exercise, you'll discover the answers to fearlessly living your truth are right there in front of you. All you have to do is tune in and listen.

Many famous businesspeople have said their intuition has been a key factor in their success—people such as Bill Gates, Steve Jobs, Oprah Winfrey, Jack Welch, and Donald Trump. People in the arts often talk about inspiration, a light going on in their head, a little nudge from within saying, "Go this way," or "Try this." We all experience these moments, it's just a matter of paying attention to them when they show up. Then, instead of applying your mental prowess to question the information you're receiving, just go with it and see where it takes you. The biggest mistake people make when it comes to their intuition or gut feeling is to ask, "Is this real, am I making this up?" Once we begin questioning, we're most likely going to get ourselves all tangled up in confusion.

Now, this is not to say that getting used to listening to your gut feelings doesn't take some practice. Like anything, we have to sharpen our skills, learn to take notice when we're getting inner messages. For most of us, it takes time and getting used to receiving what can very often be quite subtle messages. It's unlikely we're going to get the biblical version of the heavens opening and God's voice booming down calling our name, a burning bush, or even a special star shining brightly. It's going to be a little nudge, a slight feeling that could come from our stomach, a sensation in the area right between our eyebrows, a flash of insight. Or our messages could even come in the form of a dream.

However your gut feeling or intuition works for you, capitalize on it. Once you begin relying on your intuition, the next step in learning to reel in your unique power is to live big, go deep.

Live big, go deep. As a Fearless Fish out of water, you're the one changing and evolving while others are standing still trying to conform, trying hard not to stand out, making sure they don't rock the boat. Sure, it can be frustrating, even lonely sometimes, to think differently or to look different from everyone else. But to hide or wish away everything that's unique about you is energy draining and inauthentic. It's time to celebrate! You've taken the seven steps—a critical journey in which you've learned to uncover your authentic self, discovered ways your differences are attractive, found out you can align with what's familiar (your comfort zones). Now you can head out into the world with confidence!

Susan O'Meara has had a life that exemplifies being a fish out of water, overcoming obstacles—created by others and herself—and going far beyond to become someone who thrives on her uniqueness. She provides an encompassing perspective that I feel is a fitting close to *The Fearless Fish Out of Water*. Her story captures the essence of what a fish out of water can become.

I don't think it really dawned on me until I was in my 40s that being a fish out of water was such an asset. Being unique, having a unique perspective, experiencing life uniquely is what it's all about. In my 20s, following graduate school in creative writing, I took a backseat to my passions and did, what appeared to be the safe thing. I got a job to pay the rent. While friends and classmates went on to make names for themselves in the literary cosmos, I jumped ship for a regular paycheck. And I was misery personified. But I had no idea where I belonged. I just knew it wasn't at Showtime, where I eventually became a marketing manager. Then, suddenly in 1988, I'd had enough with toe-the-line culture and was ready to go out on my own.

This prompted probably the most awkward phase in my life, the most I've ever felt like a fish out of water: my transition several years ago from sunny California to moody Ireland. Talk about a transatlantic move! It was epic; it was energizing; it was eerie; it was enervating. I was a lonesome dove, a mystified alien, a gawky 40-something lost in translation, going through more of a second adolescence than a midlife crisis. All this despite the fact that my sister had moved to Dublin the year before; I had relatives in Ireland, in England, and on the Continent; and I had spent many a summer and countless holidays on the Emerald Isle. It was, in the most basic sense, my home away from home.

So I left L.A., hearth, career, beloved friends, beautiful weather year-round, a relative safety net for an often marrow-chilling, capricious, unknown, and unexpected environment. It was a greater shock to my system than I ever could have expected. Starting over in your 40s, establishing yourself, embracing yourself is much harder to do than in the more flexible, more elastic 20s and 30s. But I wanted escape into the unknown, the unfamiliar. I still don't think it's that important to fit in as much as it is to find your "people" where you add to and find a sense of belonging or community or collaboration. Fitting in is overrated; it can be the lowest common denominator. It's like squeezing yourself into a sport sock.

What I have come to know in looking back over my chaotic career is that the power plays of corporate life aren't about power at all. Because true, real, lasting power is helping people, not making them do what you want them to. It's not about getting ahead, but helping others to do that.

> *I hope I've been an agent for change in quiet, un-assuming ways; sometimes a whisper speaks louder than a shout. It's never too late to start over, start your dream, start yourself on a new, wondrous path.*

As a Fearless Fish out of water, you now know there are ways to embrace the culture of your workplace without buying in. You understand the value of advocacy for yourself and others. You appreciate what having and being a mentor can mean to your career and to the lives of others. Your fearless journey can embody these steps toward living a life where pleasure, virtue, and prosperity can all coexist.

You have so much to offer and so much to gain.

Evolution—change—in its many forms is something to welcome; it is energizing, it keeps you fresh and current. Self-acceptance, conviction, belief, courage, action, and trusting your gut are part of your new vocabulary. Shine brightly. You have so much to offer and so much to gain. Live big, go deep. Give the world a *fearless* representation of who you are. Ultimately, you'll be the one whose individuality makes a difference.

Step 7 Exercises

Find the courage to be exactly who you are.

What event happened to you as either a child or an adult that rocked your world?

_____
_____
_____
_____
_____
_____

How has this event defined you?

_____
_____
_____
_____

Make a list of what you believe about yourself.

1. _____
2. _____
3. _____
4. _____
5. _____
6. _____

Which of these are your own beliefs?

1. _____
2. _____
3. _____

Which of these are what people believe about you?

1. _____
2. _____
3. _____

Which of these beliefs is grounded in reality?

1. _____

2. _____

3. _____

List your biggest accomplishments. Next to this list, put what belief in yourself got you there.

Accomplishment   Belief

_____

_____

_____

_____

When was the last time you trusted your instincts?

_____

_____

_____

_____

What signs did you see along the way?

_____

_____

What action do you need to take now?

_____

_____

_____

_____

What does your head (intellect) say to do?

_____

_____

What does your heart (emotions) say to do?

_____

_____

What does your soul (inner knowledge) say to do?

_____

_____

How will you "live big and go deep" into your future? Paint the picture of the unique life you want.

_____

_____

_____

_____

_____

_____

_____

_____

_____

_____

Fearless Last Words

The word *fearless* was first used in popular English literature around the year 1200. Since then, and for many centuries before, man has been on a quest to face life's challenges with courage. As a fish out of water, I'm sure that you have often felt alone in this quest.

The quotes below are from the Fearless Fish interviewed for this book. Their words are here to remind you that there are others out there, just like you, who have achieved success by doing it their way. I hope their advice inspires you on your own unique journey.

"Trust in yourself and follow your passion, no matter what the odds are—even if you're alone. Real risk taking happens when we push forward to make a difference in the world."
    —**Kim Deck**, lawyer turned top employment mediator

"Stick to your dreams. Have confidence. Be silly enough to take a chance and follow your convictions."
    —**Vinnie Malcolm**, television executive

"Keep your identity, but become an American. Learn English. Learn the culture. Learn the people."
—**Zeev Haskal**, Founder of a leading investigation company

"Deliver the real deal, tell the truth, don't worry about stirring things up. Bottom line, be yourself. What you think makes you different can make you."

—**Nathalie Lubensky**, senior corporate executive

"You have to be fearless with an innate hunger in your stomach for something. But, you can't just have ambition and talent, you have to learn the tools."

—**Thom Beers**, Broadway actor turned
major television producer

"Forgive yourself and others. Embrace mistakes as the learning tools they truly are. Let the current guide you but be sure to make your own waves."

—**Susan O'Meara**, filmmaker

"You have to find what you are charged up by. If you are just grinding away the hours, you'll never succeed. Find your drive and passion . . . you'll make it."

—**Kristina Song**, cable programming executive

"Don't let society define you. Work solely based on your passions and motivations in life. Make excellence your differentiating virtue."

—**Jason Heller**, Hip-Hop record producer
turned media agency owner

"Have a point of view. Have experiences. Read books, travel, and don't go down the traditional path. Follow your interests and passions and they will take you where you want you go."

—**Erica Huggins**, film editor turned
Hollywood movie producer

"You have to be authentic. You have to accommodate to some degree the overall culture, but never stop being who you are."

>—**Graciela Meibar**, corporate diversity executive

"If you put it out there, it actually could happen. Have confidence in yourself and rely on your instincts."

>—**Kelliegh Dulany**, corporate responsibility steward

"Swim against the current if it takes you where you want to go. Don't worry about the tools you have, decide where you want to go and acquire the tools."

>—**Safia K. Rizvi, Ph.D.**, pharmaceutical executive

"Success follows commitment. You'll feel the most fortunate if your commitment helps other people. That kind of reward is very tangible."

>—**Will Halm**, Founder, National Fertility Law Center

"Expect people not to like you when you first meet them. Don't change who you are to make them like you."

>—**Roxanne "Roxy" Roffer**, 8-year-old who moved
>from Los Angeles to Santa Fe